C. H. Spurg[eon]

M000200049

Spurgeon's Sermons on
New Testament Men

Book Two

CHARLES HADDON SPURGEON

kregel
PUBLICATIONS

Grand Rapids, MI 49501

Spurgeon's Sermons on New Testament Men • Book Two

Copyright © 1996 by Kregel Publications

Published by Kregel Publications, a division of Kregel, Inc., P.O. Box 2607, Grand Rapids, MI 49501. Kregel Publications provides trusted, biblical publications for Christian growth and service. Your comments and suggestions are valued.

Cover artwork: Don Ellens
Cover and book design: Alan G. Hartman

Library of Congress Cataloging-in-Publication Data
Spurgeon, C. H. (Charles Haddon), 1834–1892.
   [Sermons on New Testament men]
   Spurgeon's sermons on New Testament men • book two / by Charles H. Spurgeon.
      p.   cm.—(C. H. Spurgeon sermon series)
   1. Men in the Bible—Biography—Sermons. 2. Bible. N.T.—Biography—Sermons. 3. Sermons, English. 4. Baptists—Sermons I. Title. II. Series: Spurgeon, C. H. (Charles Haddon), 1834–1892. C. H. Spurgeon sermon series.
BS2447.S78   1996   220.9'2'081—dc20   94-13039
                                    CIP

ISBN 0-8254-3791-1

Printed in the United States of America
1 2 3 4 5 / 00 99 98 97 96

Contents

1

John and Herod

For Herod feared John, knowing that he was a just man and an holy, and observed him; and when he heard him, he did many things, and heard him gladly (Mark 6:20).

John sought no honor among men. It was his delight to say concerning our Lord Jesus, "He must increase, but I must decrease" (John 3:30). Yet, though John sought no honor of men, he had honor. For it is written, Herod feared John. Herod was a great monarch; John was but a poor preacher whose garment and diet were of the coarsest kind—but Herod feared John. John was more royal than royal Herod. His character made him the true king, and the nominal king trembled before him. A man is not to be estimated according to his rank but according to his character. The peerage that God recognizes is arranged according to a man's justice and holiness. He is first before God and holy angels who is first in obedience. He reigns and is made a king and a priest whom God has sanctified and clothed with the fair white linen of a holy life. Be not covetous of worldly honors, for you will have honor enough even from wicked men if your lives are holiness unto the Lord.

Let it be written on John's tomb, if he needs an epitaph, "Herod feared John." Only there is one better testimonial that any minister of the Gospel might be glad to receive, and it is this: "John did no miracle: but all things that John spake of this man were true." He wrought no marvelous work that astonished his generation, but he spoke of Jesus, and all that he said was true. God grant that our Master's servants may win such praise.

My subject at this time does not lead me to speak so much of John as of Herod. I desire to have no Herod in this congregation, but I am anxious about some of you lest you should be like him. Therefore I will

---

This sermon was taken from *The Metropolitan Tabernacle Pulpit* and was preached at the Metropolitan Tabernacle, Newington.

speak out of the tenderness of my heart with the desire that none of you may follow the steps of this evil king.

The Hopeful Points in Herod's Character

Thee were several hopeful points in Herod's character. First, we find that *Herod respected justice and holiness,* for "Herod feared John, knowing that he was a just man and an holy." I like to see in every man a respect for virtue even if he himself has it not, for it may be that the next step will be to desire it, and he that desires to be just is almost so. Some have brought their minds to such a pitch of sinfulness that they despise goodness and ridicule justice and devotion. May God grant that we may never by any process be brought into such a fearful condition as that. When the conscience comes to be so confused as to lose its reverence for that which is good and holy, then is a man in a sad plight indeed. Herod was not in that condition. He honored justice, honesty, truth, courage, and purity of life. Though he had not these things himself, yet he had a salutary dread of them that is a near approach to respect for them. I know I am speaking to a great many who respect everything that is good and right; they only wish they were good and right themselves. So far, so good.

The next good point I see in Herod was that *he admired the man in whom he saw justice and righteousness,* and that is a step further. For you may admire an abstract virtue, and yet when you see it actually embodied in a man you may hate him. The ancients recognized justice in Aristides, and yet some of them grew sick of hearing him called "the just." A man may be acknowledged to be just and holy, and for that very reason he may be dreaded. You like to see lions and tigers in the zoological gardens, but you would not like to see them in your own room. You would very much prefer to view them behind bars and within cages. So very many have respect for religion, but religious people they cannot bear. They admire justice! How eloquently they speak of it, but they do not like to deal justly. They admire holiness! But if they come across a saint they persecute him. Herod feared John and tolerated John, and went the length of even keeping John for a while out of the hands of Herodias. Many of you like the company of God's people. In fact, you are out of your element when you get with the profane; you cannot endure them, and from those that practice debasing vices you fly at once. You delight in choice company. So far, so good, but that is not enough. We must go much further or else we may remain like Herod after all.

A third good point about Herod was that *he listened to John.* It is nothing wonderful that you and I should listen to sermons. But it is rather wonderful that a king should do so, and such a king as Herod. Monarchs do not often care for religious discourses except such as come from court preachers who wear fine raiment and use soft speech. John was not the kind of man for a king's palace—too rough, too blunt, too plain speaking. His words thrust too much home, yet Herod heard him gladly. It was a hopeful point in his character that he would hear a man who preached justice, holiness, and the "Lamb of God, which taketh away the sin of the world" (John 1:29). It is a fine point and a hopeful point in any man that he will hear and listen to an honest proclamation of God's Word even though it comes home to his conscience. Perhaps I address some of you who hear the Gospel only now and then, and when you drop into a religious meeting you are like the dog in the library who would gladly have changed all the books for a single bone. There are many such people in London. Religion does not suit them. Places of entertainment are much more to their minds. Some say of the preacher, "I won't hear him again; he cuts too closely; he is too personal." John said to Herod that it was not lawful for him to have his brother's wife. But, though he spoke so plainly, Herod listened to him because "he was a just man and an holy." That was well of Herod. It is well in you, my friend, if you are willing to hear the Gospel, however practically it is spoken. So far, so good.

But there was a better point still in Herod: *he obeyed the word to which he listened.* Herod heard John gladly, "And when he heard him, he did many things." Many of our hearers do nothing; they hear, they hear, they hear, and that is the end of it. They learn the way, they know the way, they are experts in the way, but they do not follow the way. They hear the Gospel invitation, but they come not to the feast. Some seem to think that religious duty lies in hearing first and talking afterward, but they are mistaken. Herod knew better than that. He was not a hearer only, he did do something, and it is remarkable that the text tells us that "he did many things." Perhaps these were some of the many things—he discharged a tax-gatherer who imposed upon the people or righted the wrongs of a neglected widow or altered a cruel law that he had promulgated or changed his habits and manners in certain respects. Certainly in many points he was an improved man, for John the Baptist had an influence with him for good, "For Herod feared John, and when he heard him, he did many things." I am speaking to some who, when they hear a sermon, put a part of it into practice, and they have done many things since they first attended here, for that we are very grateful. I have known a man who became charmed with the Gospel. He gave up his drunkenness, his Sabbath breaking. He tried, and succeeded, in a great measure, in leaving off profane language, and thus he was greatly improved. And yet, and yet he is only a Herod after all. For Herod was Herod, after he had done many things. In his heart, he was still prepared for all sorts of wickedness. Yet he did amend somewhat, and so far, so good.

There was another point about Herod, namely, that *he continued to hear the preacher gladly*. It is put into the end of the verse as if to indicate that he heard John still. John touched his conscience, but after all, he still heard him gladly. He said, "Send for John the Baptist again." Harry VIII would listen to Hugh Latimer though he denounced him to his face. He even sent him on his birthday a handkerchief on which was marked the text, "Whoremongers and adulterers God will judge." Hal cried, "Let us hear honest Hugh Latimer." Even bad men admire those who tell them truth. However unwelcome the warning, they believe it to be honestly spoken, and therefore they respect the preacher. A good point this. You who are present and unconverted have heard most cutting sentences from me, you have heard of judgment to come, and of that eternal wrath which rests upon those who die in their sins: let me warn you then, that if, after hearing the denunciations of God's Word, you are still willing to hear, I have great hopes of you. So far, so good.

There was yet one other point about Herod, and that is *his conscience was greatly affected* through the preaching of John. For I am inclined to think that a certain translation that renders the passage "Herod did many things" in another way may be a correct one: "Herod was much perplexed," or, "Herod was made to hesitate." Such a sense is found in some manuscripts. He loved his sin but could see a "beauty of holiness" in religion, and he wished to be holy. But there was Herodias, and he could not give her up. When he heard a sermon, he was like a relative of his in after days, almost persuaded, yet he did not give up his lust. He could not go the whole length John would have him go. He could not leave his bosom sin, and yet he felt as if he wished to leave it. There was a halting between two opinions, a hesitating, a wavering. He was inclined to good if he could have good and have his pleasure too. But his pleasure was so very much his master that he could not escape from it. He was like a bird taken with lime twigs. He wanted to fly, but, sad to say, he was willingly held, limed by his lust. This is the case with many of our hearers. Their consciences are not weaned from their sins. They cannot give them up, and yet they wish they could. They linger on the brink and fear to launch away. They are almost out of Sodom, have almost escaped the fire shower, and yet in all probability they will stand like Lot's wife, a pillar of salt, because they will look back and love the sin that lingers in their hearts. Consciences nowadays seem to have gone out of fashion, but to have a conscience sensitive to the preaching of the Word is an admirable thing. If you have such a thing, so far, so good.

There were six good points about Herod, then. But now, very sorrowfully, I want to indicate the flaws.

The Flaws in the Case of Herod

The first flaw was this, that *though he loved John, he never looked to John's Master.* John never wanted anybody to be his disciple, but he cried, "Behold the Lamb of God." Herod was, after a sort, a follower of John but never a follower of Jesus. It is easy for you to hear the preacher and love him and admire him, and yet the preacher's Master may be all unknown to you. I pray you, dear friends, do not let this be the case with any of you. I am the bridegroom's friend, and I shall rejoice greatly when the bridegroom wins your hearts. God forbid that I through my ministry should ever lead you to myself and cause you to stop there. We are only signposts pointing to Christ. Go beyond us. Be followers of us as far as we are followers of Christ but in no other respect. It is to Christ you must go. The end of all our ministry is Christ Jesus. We want you to go to Him direct, to seek from Him pardon, from Him redemption, from Him a change of heart, from Him a new life, for vain will it be if you have listened to the most faithful of preachers and have not listened to the preacher's Master and obeyed His Gospel. You will be Herods and nothing more, unless grace leads you to Jesus Christ.

The second flaw about Herod's case was that *he had no respect for goodness in his own heart.* He admired it in another, but there was none of it in himself. Our Savior described Herod admirably. What a master sketcher of human portraits was Christ! He said of Herod, "Go ye, and tell that fox" (Luke 13:32). Herod was a foxy man, selfish, full of tricks—timid when he was in the presence of his superiors—but both cruel and bold when he was in the presence of those who could not defend themselves. We sometimes meet with these foxy people. They want to go to heaven, but they like the road to hell. They will sing a hymn to Jesus, but a good roaring song they like also when they get merry companions together. By all manner of means, give a guinea to the church. Oh, yes! admirable thing. But how many guineas are spent upon some secret lust? So many try to dodge between God and Satan. They do not want to fall foul of either; they hold with the hare and run with the hounds. They admire all that is good, but they do not want to have too much of it themselves. It might be inconvenient to carry the Cross of Christ on their own shoulders and become precise and exact in their own lives, yet they never say a word against other people doing so. It is a fatal flaw to have no root in yourself—a damning flaw, condemning your own self—to know the right and disregard it, to feel respect for it and yet trample it under foot. I judge that the doom of such will be far more dreadful than that of those who never knew the good, who were trained up in the purlieus of vice, and who never had a glimpse of holiness and purity and therefore never deliberately turned away from them.

Another flaw in Herod's character was that *he never loved the Word of God as God's word.* He admired John and probably said, "That is the man for me. See how boldly he delivers his Master's message. That is the man I should like to hear." But he never said to himself, "God sent John; God speaks to me through John. Oh, that I might learn what John is speaking and be instructed and improved by the word John is uttering, because it is God's word." No, no. I do pray you, ask yourselves, dear hearers, whether this may not apply to you. May it not be that you listen to a sermon because it is Mr. So-and-so's discourse, and you admire the preacher? It will be fatal to you if you treat the Word in that way. It must be to you what it is in truth, the Word of God, or it will not save you. It will never impress your soul unless you accept it as the Word of God, bow before it, and desire to feel all its power as coming to you fresh from the lips of God and sent into your heart by His Holy Spirit.

Now, we know Herod did not receive the word as the Word of God because he was a picker and chooser in reference to it. He did not like John's discourse when he spoke of the seventh commandment. If he spoke of the fourth commandment he would say, "That is admirable; the Jews ought to keep it." But when he dealt with the seventh commandment, Herod and Herodias would say, "We do not think preachers should allude to such subjects." I have always noticed that people who live in the practice of vice think the servants of God ought not to allude to things so coarse. We are allowed to denounce the sins of the man in the moon and the vices of savages in the middle of Africa. But as to the everyday vices of this city of London, if we put a finger upon them in God's name, then straightway someone cries, "It is indelicate to allude to these things." John dealt with the whole Word of God. He did not only say, "Behold the Lamb of God," but he cried, "The axe is laid unto the root of the trees" (Luke 3:9). He spoke plainly to the conscience. Herod, therefore, had this fatal flaw in his character that he did not attend to all that John delivered of the Word of God. He liked one part and did not like another. He resembled those who prefer a doctrinal discourse but cannot endure the precepts of God's Word. I hear one exclaim, "I like practical discourses. I do not want any doctrine." Don't you? There is doctrine in God's Word and you are to receive what God gives you—not half a Bible, but the whole truth as it is in Jesus. That was a great fault in Herod. He did not receive the testimony of John as the Word of God.

Next, *Herod did many things but he did not do all things.* He who receives the Word of God in truth does not only attempt to do many things, but he tries to do all that is right. He does not give up one vice or a dozen vices, but he endeavors to forsake every false way and seeks to be delivered from every iniquity. Herod did not care for a thorough reformation, for that would call for too great a self-denial. He had one sin he wished to keep, and when John spoke plainly about that he would not listen to him.

Another fault with Herod was that *he was under the sway of sin.* He had given himself up to Herodias. She was his own niece, had been married to his own brother, and was the mother of children by his own brother. Yet he led her away from his own brother's house that she might become his wife, he himself casting off one who had been a good and faithful wife to him for years. It is a mess of filthy incest one hardly likes to think of. The influence of this woman was his curse and ruin. How many men have been destroyed in that way! How many women are ruined daily in this city by coming under the vicious influence of others! My dear men and women, you will have to stand before God on your own account. Do not let anyone cast a spell over you. I pray you, escape for your life; run for it when vice hunts you. I may be sent at this moment with a word on purpose for you, to stir up your conscience and arouse you to a sense of your danger. It is always perilous to be under the influence of an unconverted person, however moral he may be, but it is supremely dangerous to be under the fascination of a wicked woman or a vicious man. God help you to rise above it by His Spirit, for if you are hearers of the Word and doers of evil, you will end in being Herods and nothing more.

I will only allude to another point in Herod's character, that *his religion,* although it made him do many things, *was rather one of fear than of love.* It is not said that Herod feared God but that he feared *John.* He did not love John; he feared John. The whole thing was a matter of fear. He was not a lion, you see. He was a fox—fearful, timid, ready to run away from every barking cur.

There are many people whose whole religion lies in fear. With some it is the fear of men: the fear of what people would say if they did not pretend to be religious, the fear of what their Christian associates would think of them if they were not reputable. With others there is the fear that some awful judgment would come upon them. But the mainspring of the religion of Christ is love. Oh! to love the Gospel, to delight in the truth, to rejoice in holiness—this is genuine conversion. The fear of death and the fear of hell create a poor, poor faith that leaves men on Herod's level still.

What Became of Herod

With all his good points, Herod ended most wretchedly. First, *he slew the preacher whom he once respected.* It was he who did it, though the executioner was the instrument. He said, "Go and fetch John the

Baptist's head in a charger." So it has happened with many hopeful hearers. They have become slanderers and persecutors of the very preachers before whom they once trembled, and far as they could they have taken off their heads. After a time men dislike being rebuked, and they proceed in their dislike until they scoff at the things they once reverenced and make the name of Christ a football for their jests. Beware! I pray you, beware! for the way of sin is downhill. Herod feared John, and yet he beheaded him. A person may be evangelical and Calvinistic, and so on, yet, if he is placed under certain conditions, he may become a hater and a persecutor of the truth he once avowed.

Herod went a step lower, however. For this *Herod Antipas was the man who afterward mocked the Savior.* It is said, "Herod with his men of war set him at nought, and mocked him, and arrayed him in a gorgeous robe" (Luke 23:11). This is the man that "did many things" under the leading of John. His course is altered now. He spits on the Redeemer and insults the Son of God. Certain of the most outrageous blasphemers of the Gospel were originally Sunday school scholars and teachers, young men who were almost persuaded. Yet they halted and hesitated and wavered until they made the plunge and became much worse than they possibly could have become if they had not seen the light of truth. If the Devil wants raw material to make a Judas, the son of perdition, he takes an apostle to work upon. When he takes a thoroughly bad character like Herod, it is necessary to make him plastic as Herod had been in the hands of John. Somehow or other, border men are the worst enemies. In the old wars between England and Scotland, the borders were the fighting men; so the border people will do more harm than any until we get them on this side of the frontier. Oh, that the grace of God may decide those who now hesitate!

I may mention to you that, before long, *Herod lost all the power he possessed.* He was a foxy man and always tried to win power, but in the end he was recalled by the Roman emperor in disgrace. That was the end of him. Many a man has given up Christ for honor and has lost himself as well as lost Christ, like the man who, in the old Catholic persecuting times, was brought to prison for the faith. He said he loved the Protestant faith, but he cried, "I cannot burn." So he denied the faith, and in the dead of night his house took fire. The man who could not burn was forced to burn, but he had no comfort in that burning, for he had denied his Lord. If you sell Christ for a mess of pottage it will scald your lips; it will burn within your soul like molten lead forever—"the wages of sin is death" (Rom. 6:23). However bright the golden coin shines and however musical may be its chink, it will prove an awful curse to the man who sells his Lord to gain it.

Today *the name of Herod is infamous forever*. As long as there is a Christian church, the name of Herod will be execrated. And is it not a solemn reflection that "Herod feared John, . . . and . . . did many things, and heard him gladly"? I know that no young man here believes that he will ever turn out to be a Herod. I might, like the prophet, say, "Thou wilt do this, and do that" (2 Kings 8:13). And you would answer, "Is thy servant a dog, that he should do this great thing?" But you will do it, unless you are decided for God.

An appeal like this once startled me. When I was young and tender, there was a hopeful youth who went to school with me who was held up to me as an example. He was a good boy. I used to feel no particular affection for his name because I was so perpetually chided by his goodness, and I was so far removed from it. Being younger than he, I saw him enter upon his apprenticeship, enter upon the merriment of a great city, and come back dishonored. It horrified me. Might not I dishonor my character? And when I found that if I gave myself to Christ He would give me a new heart and a right spirit and when I read that promise of the covenant, "I will put my fear in their hearts, that they shall not depart from me" (Jer. 32:40), it seemed to me like a Character Insurance Society. If I believed in Jesus Christ my character was insured. Christ would enable me to walk in the paths of holiness. This charmed me into desiring an interest in Christ.

If you would not like to be a Herod, be a disciple of Jesus Christ. There will be no choice for some of you. Some of you are of such powerful natures that you must either thoroughly serve Christ or serve the Devil. An old Scotchman was once looking at Rowland Hill, and the good old gentleman said, "What are you looking at?" He said, "The lines of your face." "What do you think of them?" He replied, "I think that if you had not been a Christian man, you would have been an awful sinner." Some people are of that sort. They are like a pendulum, they must swing one way or the other. Oh, that you may swing Christ's way tonight. Cry, "Lord, help me to cleanse my way. Help me to be wholly Yours. Help me to possess the righteousness I admire, the holiness I respect. Help me not only to do some things, but everything You would have me to do. Take me, make me Yours. I will rejoice and joy in Him who helps me to be holy." God bless you, dear friends, for Jesus Christ's sake. Amen.

2

Andrew:
Everyday Usefulness

And he brought him to Jesus (John 1:42).

We have a most intense desire for the revival of religion in our own midst and throughout all the churches of our Lord Jesus. We see that error is making great advances, and we would fain lift up a banner for the cause of truth. We pity the mighty populations among whom we dwell, for they are still godless and Christless. The things of their peace are hid from their eyes, therefore would we fain behold the Lord performing miracles of grace. Our hope is that the set time to favor Zion is come, and we intend to be importunate in prayer that God will reveal His arm and do great things in these latter days. Our eager desire, of which our special services will be the expression, is a right one. Challenge it who will, be it ours to cultivate it and prove by our zeal for God that the desire is not insincere or superficial.

But, my brethren, it is very possible that in addition to cultivating a vehement desire for the revival of religion, we may have been daydreaming and forecasting in our minds a conception of the form that the divine visitation shall take. Remembering what we have heard of former times of refreshing, you expect a repetition of the same outward signs and look for the Lord to work as He did with Livingstone at the Kirk of Shotts or with Jonathan Edwards in New England or Whitefield in our own land. Perhaps you have planned in your mind that God will raise up an extraordinary preacher whose ministry will attract the multitude, and while he is preaching, God the Holy Spirit will attend the Word so that hundreds will be converted under every sermon. Other evangelists will be raised up of a like spirit and from end to end this island shall hear the truth and feel its power.

This sermon was taken from *The Metropolitan Tabernacle Pulpit* and was preached on Sunday morning, February 14, 1869.

14

Now it may be that God will so visit us. It may be that such signs and wonders as have frequently attended revivals may be again witnessed—the Lord may rend the heavens and come out and make the mountains to flow down at His feet. But it is just possible that He may select quite another method. His Holy Spirit may reveal Himself like a mighty river swollen with floods and sweeping all before its majestic current. But if so He wills, He may rather unveil His power as the gentle dew that, without observation, refreshes all the earth. It may happen to us as to Elias when the fire and the wind passed before him, but the Lord was not in either of those mighty agencies. He preferred to commune with His servant in a still, small voice. Perhaps that still, small voice is to be language of grace in this congregation. It will be useless then for us to be mapping out the way of the eternal God, idle for us to be rejecting all the good that He may be pleased to give us because it does not happen to come in the shape that we have settled in our own minds to be the proper one. Idle, did I say? Such prejudice would be wicked in the extreme.

It has very frequently happened that while men have been sketching out imaginary designs, they have missed actual opportunities. They would not build because they could not erect a palace. They therefore shiver in the winter's cold. They would not be clothed in homespun, for they looked for scarlet and fine linen before long. They were not content to do a little and therefore did nothing. I want, therefore, to say this morning to every believer here, it is vain for us to be praying for an extensive revival of religion and comforting each other in the hope of it, if meanwhile we suffer our zeal to effervesce and sparkle and then to be dissipated. Our proper plan is written, with the highest expectations, "She hath done what she could" (Mark 14:8), by laboring diligently in such holy works as may be within our reach, according to Solomon's precept: "Whatsoever thy hand findeth to do, do it with thy might" (Eccl. 9:10). While believers are zealously doing what God enables them to do, they are in the high road to abundant success. But if they stand all the day idle, gaping after wonders, their spiritual want shall come upon them as an armed man.

I have selected the text before us in order that I may speak upon matters practical and efforts within the reach of all. We shall not speak of the universal triumph of the Gospel but of its victory in single hearts, nor shall we deal with the efforts of an entire church but with the pious fervor of individual disciples. If the Christian church were in a proper and healthy state, the members would be so studious of the Word of God and would themselves have so much of the Spirit of Christ that the only thing they would need in the great assemblies, over and above worship, would be a short encouraging and animating word of direction addressed to them—as to well-drilled and enthusiastic soldiers who need but the word of command, and the deed of valor is straightway performed. So would I speak and so would I have you hear at this hour.

Coming then to the subject, Andrew was converted by Christ to become His disciple. Immediately he sets to work to recruit the little army by discipling others. He finds his brother Peter and brings him to Jesus.

The Commonplace Disciple

Andrew is the picture of what all disciples of Christ should be. To begin, then, this first successful Christian missionary was himself *a sincere follower of Jesus*. Is it needful to make the observation? No—will it ever be needless while so many make a profession of a faith that they do not possess? When so many will wantonly thrust themselves into the offices of Christ's church, having no concern for the glory of His kingdom and no part or lot in it, it will be always needful to repeat that warning, "Unto the wicked God saith, What hast thou to do to declare my statutes?" (Ps. 50:16). Men who have never seen the beauties of Emmanuel are not fit persons to describe them to others. An experimental acquaintance with vital godliness is the first necessity for a useful worker for Jesus. That preacher is accursed who knows not Christ for himself. God may, in infinite sovereignty, make him the means of blessing to others. But every moment that he tarries in the pulpit he is an impostor; every time he preaches he is a mocker of God. Woe to him when his Master calls him to His dread account. You unconverted young people who enter upon the work of Sunday school instruction, and so undertake to teach to others what you do not know yourselves, do place yourselves in a position of unusual solemnity and of extraordinary peril. I say, of extraordinary peril, because you do by the fact of being a teacher profess to know and you will be judged by your profession—I fear condemned out of your own mouths.

You know the theory only of religion, and of what use is that while you are strangers to its power? How can you lead others along a way that you yourself refuse to tread? Besides, I have noticed that persons who become active in church work before they have first believed in Christ are very apt to remain without faith, resting content with the general repute that they have gained. O dear friends, beware of this. In this day hypocrisy is so common, self-deceit is so easy, that I would not have you place yourselves where those vices become almost inevitable. If a man voluntarily puts himself where it is taken for granted that he is godly, his next step will be to mimic godliness. By and by he will flatter himself into the belief that he really possesses that which he so successfully imitates. Beware, dear hearer, of a religion that is not true. It is worse than none. Beware of a form of godliness that is not supported by the fervor of your heart and soul. This age of shams presents but few assistances to self-examination, hence am I the more earnest that every one of us, before he shall seek to bring others to Christ, should deliberately ask himself, Am I a follower of Christ myself? Am I washed in His blood? Am I renewed by His Spirit? If not, my first business is not in the pulpit, but on my knees in prayer. My first occupation should not be in the Sunday school class but in my closet, confessing my sin and seeking pardon through the atoning sacrifice.

Andrew was earnest for the souls of others, though he was but *a young convert*. So far as I can gather, he appears to have beheld Jesus as the Lamb of God one day and to have found out his brother Peter the next. Far be it from us to forbid you who but yesterday found joy and peace to exert your newborn zeal and youthful ardor. No, my brethren and sisters, delay not, but make haste to spread abroad the good news that is now so fresh and so full of joy to you. It is right that the advanced and the experienced should be left to deal with the captious and the skeptical. But you, even you, young as you are, may find some with whom you can cope, some brother like Simon Peter, some sister dear to you who will listen to your unvarnished tale and believe in your simple testimony. Though you be but young in grace and but little instructed, begin the work of soulwinning, and

> Tell to sinners round
> What a dear Savior you have found.

If the religion of Jesus Christ consisted in doctrines hard to be understood, if the saving truths of Christianity were metaphysical points difficult to handle, then a matured judgment would be needed in every worker for God. It would be prudent to say to the young convert, "Hold back until you are instructed." But since that which saves souls is as simple as A B C, since it is nothing but this: "He that believeth and is baptized shall be saved," he that trusts the merit of Christ shall be saved. You who have trusted Him know that He saves you, and you know that He will save others. I charge you before God, tell it, tell it right and left, but especially tell it to your own kinsfolk and acquaintance that they also may find eternal life.

Andrew was a disciple, a new disciple and, I may add, *a commonplace disciple*, a man of average capacity. He was not at all the brilliant character that Simon Peter, his brother, turned out to be. Throughout the life of Jesus Christ, Andrew's name occurs, but no notable incident is connected therewith. Though in afterlife he no doubt became a most useful apostle and, according to tradition, sealed his life's ministry by death upon a cross, yet at the first Andrew was, as to talent, an ordinary believer—one of that common standard and nothing remarkable. Yet

Andrew became a useful minister, and thus it is clear that servants of Jesus Christ are not to excuse themselves from endeavoring to extend the boundaries of His kingdom by saying, "I have no remarkable talent or singular ability." I very much disagree with those who decry ministers of slender gifts, sneering at them as though they ought not to occupy the pulpit at all. Are we, after all, brethren, as servants of God to be measured by mere oratorical ability? Is this after the fashion of Paul when he renounced the wisdom of words lest the faith of the disciples should stand in the wisdom of man and not in the power of God? If you could blot out from the Christian church all the minor stars and leave nothing but those of the first magnitude, the darkness of this poor world would be increased sevenfold. How often the eminent preachers that are the church's delight are brought into the church by those of less degree, even as Simon Peter was converted by Andrew! Who shall tell what might have become of Simon Peter if it had not been for Andrew? Who shall say that the church would ever have possessed a Peter if she had closed the mouth of Andrew? And who shall put a finger upon the brother or sister of inferior talent and say, "These must hold their peace"? No, brother, if you have but one talent, the more zealously use it. God will require it of you. Let not your family or friends hold you back from putting it out to interest. If you are but as a glowworm's lamp, hide not your light, for there is an eye predestinated to see by your light, a heart ordained to find comfort by your faint gleam. Shine and the Lord accept you.

I am putting it in this way that I may come to the conclusion that every single professor of the faith of Christ is bound to do something for the extension of the Redeemer's kingdom. I would that all the members of this church, whatever their talents are, would be like Andrew in promptness. He is no sooner a convert than he is a missionary, no sooner taught than he begins to teach. I would have them, like Andrew, persevering as well as prompt. He first finds Peter—that is his first success. But how many afterward he found, who shall tell? Throughout a long life of usefulness it is probable that Andrew brought many stray sheep to the Redeemer's fold, yet certainly that first one would be among the dearest to his heart. He first findeth Peter. He was the spiritual father of many sons, but he rejoiced most that he was the father of his own brother Peter—his brother in the flesh but his son in Christ Jesus.

Could it be possible for me to come to every one of you personally and grasp you by the hand, I would with most affectionate earnestness—yes, even with tears—pray you by Him to whom you owe your souls, awake and render personal service to the Lover of your souls. Make no excuse, for no excuse can be valid from those who are bought with so great a price. Your business, you will tell me, requires so much of your thoughts—I know it does. Then use your business in such a way as to serve God in it. Still there must be some scraps of time that you could devote to holy service. There must be some opportunities for directly aiming at conversions. I charge you avail yourselves of such occasions, lest they be laid to your door. To some of you the excuse of business does not apply, for you have seasons of leisure. Oh, I beseech you, let not that leisure be driveled away in frivolities, in mere talk, in sleep and self-indulgence! Let not time slip away in vain persuasions that you can do nothing or in the mere preparations for grand experiments, but now, like Andrew, hasten at once to serve Jesus. If you can reach but one individual, let him not remain unsought. Time is hastening and men are perishing. The world is growing old in sin. Superstition and idolatry root themselves into the very soul of human nature. When, when will the church become intent upon putting down her Master's foes? Possessing such little strength, we cannot afford to waste a jot of it. With such awful demands upon us we cannot afford to trifle.

O that I had the power to stir the hearts and souls of all my fellow Christians by a description of this huge city wallowing in iniquity, by a picture of the graveyards and cemeteries fattening on innumerable corpses, by a portrayal of that lake of fire to which multitudes yearly descend. Surely sin, the grave, and hell are themes that might create a tingling even in the dull, cold ear of death. O that I could set before you the Redeemer upon the cross dying to ransom souls! O that I could depict the heaven that sinners lose and their remorse when they shall find themselves self-excluded! I wish I could even set before you in vivid light the cases of your own sons and daughters, the spiritual condition of your own brothers and sisters: without Christ, therefore without hope, unrenewed, and therefore heirs of wrath even as others. Then might I expect to move each believer here to an immediate effort to pluck men as brands from the burning.

His Great Object

The great object of Andrew seems to have been to bring Peter to Jesus. This, too, should be the aim of every renewed heart—to bring our friends to *Jesus*, not to convert them to a party. There are certain unbrotherly sectarians, called Brethren, who compass sea and land to make proselytes from other churches. These are not merchants seeking goodly pearls in a legitimate fashion but pirates who live by plunder. They must not excite our wrath so much as our pity, though it is difficult not to mingle with it something of disgust. While this world remains so wicked as it is, we need not be spending our strength as Christian denominations in attacking one another. It will be better for us to go and fight with the Canaanites than with rival tribes that should be one united Israel.

I should reckon it to be a burning disgrace if it could be said, "The large church under that man's pastoral care is composed of members whom he has stolen away from other Christian churches." No, but I value beyond all price the godless, the careless who are brought out from the world into communion with Christ. These are true prizes, not stealthily removed from friendly shores, but captured at the edge of the sword from an enemy's dominions. We welcome brethren and sisters from other churches if in the providence of God they are drifted to our shores. But we would never hang out the wrecker's beacon to dash other churches in pieces in order to enrich ourselves with the wreck. Far rather would we be looking after perishing souls than cajoling unstable ones from their present place of worship. To recruit one regiment from another is no real strengthening of the army; to bring in fresh men should be the aim of all.

Furthermore, the object of the soulwinner is not to bring men to an outward religiousness merely. Little will you have done for a man if you merely make the Sabbath breaker into a Sabbath keeper and leave him a self-righteous pharisee. Little will you have done for him if you persuade him, having been prayerless, to be a mere user of a form of prayer, his heart not being in it. You do but change the form of sin in which the man lives. You prevent him from being drowned in the salt water, but you throw him into the fresh. You take one poison from him, but you expose him to another. The fact is, if you would do real service to Christ, your prayer and your zeal must follow the person who has become the object of your attention until you bring him absolutely to close with grace and lay hold on Jesus Christ and accept eternal life as it is found in the atoning sacrifice. Anything short of this may have its usefulness for this world but must be useless for the world to come. To bring men to Jesus—O, be this your aim and mine!—not to bring them to baptism nor to the meeting house nor to adopt our form of worship, but to bring them to His dear feet who alone can say, Go in peace; thy sins which are many are all forgiven thee.

Friends, as we believe Jesus to be the very center of the Christian religion, he who gets not to Christ gets not to true godliness at all. Some are quite satisfied if they get to the priest and obtain his absolution, if they get the sacraments and eat bread in the church, if they get to prayers and pass through a religious routine. But we know that all this is less than nothing and vanity unless the heart draws near to Jesus. Unless the soul accepts Jesus as God's appointed sin offering and rests alone in Him, it walks in a vain show and disquiets itself in vain. Come then, friends, nerve yourselves to this point, that from this day forth let your one ambition be in dealing with your fellow men to bring them to Jesus Christ Himself. Be it determined in your spirit that you will never cease to labor for them until you have reason to believe that they are trusting in Jesus, loving Jesus, serving Jesus, united to Jesus, in the hope that they shall be conformed to the image of Jesus and dwell with Him, world without end.

But some will say, "We can very clearly understand how Andrew brought Peter to the Lord because Jesus was here among men, and they could walk together until they found him." Yes, but Jesus is not dead, and it is a mistake to suppose that He is not readily to be reached. Prayer is a messenger that can find Jesus at any hour. Jesus is gone up on high as to His body, but His spiritual presence remains to us. The Holy Spirit as the head of this dispensation is always near at hand to every believer. Intercede, then, for your friends. Plead with Christ on their account. Mention their names in your constant prayers. Set apart special times in which you plead with God for them. Let your dear sister's case ring in the ears of the Mediator. Let your dear child's name be repeated again and again in your intercessions. As Abraham pleaded for Ishmael, so let your cry come up for those who are around you that the Lord would be pleased to visit them in His mercy. Intercession is a true bringing of souls to Christ, and this means will avail when you are shut out from employing any other. If your dear ones are in Australia, in some settler's hut where even a letter cannot reach them, prayer can find them out. No ocean can be too wide for prayer to span, no distance too great for prayer to travel. Far off as they are, you can take them up in the arms of believing prayer and bear them to Jesus and say, "Master, have mercy upon them." Here is a valuable weapon for those who cannot preach or teach: they can wield the sword of all-prayer. When hearts are too hard for sermons and when good advice is rejected, it still remains to love to be allowed to plead with God for its wayward one. Tears and weepings are prevalent at the mercy seat. If *we* prevail there, the Lord will be sure to manifest His prevailing grace in obdurate spirits.

To bring men to Jesus you can adopt the next means with most of them, namely that of instructing them or putting them in the way of being informed concerning the Gospel. It is a very wonderful thing that while to us the light of the Gospel is so abundant, it should be so very partially distributed in this country. When I have expounded my own hope in Christ to two or three in a railway carriage, I have found myself telling my listeners perfect novelties. I have seen the look of astonishment upon the face of many an intelligent Englishman when I have explained the doctrine of the substitutionary sacrifice of Christ. Persons who have even attended their parish church from their youth up, I have met with who were totally ignorant of the simple truth of justification by faith. Aye, and some who have been to dissenting places of worship do not seem to have laid hold of the fundamental truth that no man is saved by his own doings but that salvation is procured by faith in the blood and righteousness of Jesus Christ. This nation is steeped up to the throat in self-righteous doctrine, and the Protestantism of Martin Luther is very generally unknown. The truth is held by as many as God's grace has called, but the great outlying world still talk of doing your best and then hoping in God's mercy—I know not what beside of legal self-confidence—while the master doctrine that he who believes in Jesus is saved by Jesus' finished work is sneered at as enthusiasm or attacked as leading to licentiousness. Tell it, then, tell it on all sides, take care that none under your influence shall be left in ignorance of it. I can bear personal witness that the statement of the Gospel has often proved in God's hand enough to lead a soul into immediate peace.

Not many months ago I met with a lady holding sentiments of almost undiluted popery, and in conversing with her I was delighted to see how interesting and attractive a thing the Gospel was to her. She complained that she enjoyed no peace of mind as the result of her religion and never seemed to have done enough. She had a high idea of priestly absolution, but it had evidently been quite unable to yield repose to her spirit. Death was feared, God was terrible, even Christ an object of awe rather than love. When I told her that whosoever believes on Jesus is perfectly forgiven and that I knew I was forgiven—that I was as sure of it as of my own existence—that I feared neither to live nor to die, for it would be the same to me because God had given me eternal life in His Son, I saw that a new set of thoughts were astonishing her mind. She said, "If I could believe that, I should be the happiest person in the world." I did not deny the inference but claimed to have proved its truth. I have reason to believe that the little simple talk we had has not been forgotten. You cannot tell how many may be in bondage for want of the simplest possible instruction upon the plainest truths of the Gospel of Jesus Christ.

Many, too, may be brought to Christ through your example. Believe me, there is no preaching in this world like the preaching of a holy life. It shames me sometimes and weakens me in my testimony for my Master when I stand here and recollect that some professors of religion are a disgrace not only to their religion, but even to common morality. It makes me feel as though I must speak with bated breath and trembling knees when I remember the damnable hypocrisy of those who thrust themselves into the church of God and by their abominable sins bring disgrace upon the cause of God and eternal destruction upon themselves. In proportion as a church is holy, in that proportion will its testimony for Christ be powerful. Oh, were the saints immaculate, our testimony would be like fire among the stubble, like the flaming firebrand in the midst of the sheaves of corn. Were the saints of God less like the world, more disinterested, more prayerful, more godlike, the tramp of the armies of Zion would shake the nations, and the day of the victory of Christ would surely dawn. Freely might the church barter her most golden-mouthed preacher if she received in exchange men of apostolic life. I would be content that the pulpit should be empty if all the members of the church would preach Jesus by their patience in suffering, by their endurance in temptation, by exhibiting in the household those graces that adorn the Gospel of Jesus Christ. Oh! so live, I pray you, in God's fear and by the Spirit's power that they who see you may ask, "Whence hath this man this holiness?" and may follow you until they are led by you to Jesus Christ to learn the secret by which men live to God. You can bring men to Jesus by your example, then.

And once again, let me say before I close this point, our object should be to bring men to Jesus, having tried intercession and instruction and example, by occasionally, as time and opportunity may serve us, giving a word of importunate entreaty. Half a dozen words from a tender mother to a boy who is just leaving home for an apprenticeship may drop like gentle dew from heaven upon him. A few sentences from a kind and prudent father given to the daughter still unconverted as she enters upon her married life and to her husband, kindly and affectionately put, may make that household forever a house for God. A kind word dropped by a brother to a sister, a little letter written from a sister to her brother, though it should be only a line or two, may be God's arrow of grace. I have known even such little things as a tear or an anxious glance to work wonders.

You perhaps may have heard the story of Mr. Whitefield, who made it his wont wherever he stayed to talk to the members of the household about their souls—with each one personally. But stopping at a certain house with a colonel who was all that could be wished except a Christian, he was so pleased with the hospitality he received and so charmed with the general character of the good colonel and his wife and daughters that he did not like to speak to them about decision as he would have done if they had been less amiable characters. He had stopped with them for a week, and during the last night the Spirit of God visited him so that he could not sleep. "These people," said he, "have been very kind to me, and I have not been faithful to them. I must do it before I go. I must tell them that whatever good thing they have, if they do not believe in Jesus they are lost." He arose and prayed. After praying he still felt contention in his spirit. His old nature said, "I cannot do it." But the Holy Spirit seemed to say, "Leave them not without warning." At last he thought of a device and prayed God to accept it. He wrote upon a diamond-shaped pane of glass in the window with his ring these words: "One thing thou lackest." He could not bring himself to speak to them but went his way with many a prayer for their conversion. He had no sooner gone than the good woman of the house, who was a great admirer of him, said, "I will go up to his room. I like to look at the very place where the man of God has been." She went up and noticed on the windowpane those words, "One thing thou lackest." It struck her with conviction in a moment. "Ah!" said she, "I thought he did not care much about us, for I knew he always pleaded with those with whom he stopped. When I found that he did not do so with us, I thought we had vexed him. But I see how it was; he was too tender in mind to speak to us." She called her daughters up. "Look there, girls," said she, "see what Mr. Whitefield has written on the window, 'One thing thou lackest.' Call up your father." And the father came up and read that too, "One thing thou lackest." Around the bed whereof the man of God had slept they all knelt down and sought that God would give them the one thing they lacked. Before they left that chamber they had found that one thing, and the whole household rejoiced in Jesus.

It is not long ago since I met with a friend one of whose church members preserves that very pane of glass in her family as an heirloom. Now, if you cannot admonish and warn in one way, do it in another. But take care to clear your soul of the blood of your relatives and friends so that it may never crimson your skirts and accuse you before God's bar. So live and speak and teach by some means or other that you shall be faithful to God and faithful to the souls of men.

His Wise Methods

I have trenched upon this subject already, but I could not help it. Andrew being zealous was *wise*. Earnestness often gives prudence and puts a man in the possession of tact if not of talent. *Andrew used what ability he had.* If he had been as some young men are of my acquaintance, he would have said, "I would like to serve God. How I would like to preach! And I would require a large congregation." Well, there is a pulpit in every street in London. There is a most wide and effectual door for preaching in this great city of ours, beneath God's blue sky. But this young zealot would rather prefer an easier berth than the open air, and, because he is not invited to the largest pulpits, does nothing. How much better it would be if, like Andrew, he began to use the ability he has among those who are accessible to him and from that stepped to something else and from that to something else, advancing year by year! Sirs, if Andrew had not been the means of converting his brother, the probabilities are that he never would have been an apostle.

Christ had some reason in the choice of His apostles to their office, and perhaps the ground of His choice of Andrew as an apostle was this: "He is an earnest man," said He. "He brought me Simon Peter. He is always speaking privately to individuals. I will make an apostle of him."

Now, you young men, if you become diligent in tract distribution, diligent in the Sunday school, you are likely men to be made into ministers. But if you stop and do nothing until you can do everything, you will remain useless—an impediment to the church instead of being a help to her. Dear sisters in Jesus Christ, you must none of you dream that you are in a position in which you can do nothing at all. That were such a mistake in providence as God cannot commit. You must have some talent entrusted to you and something given you to do that no one else can do. Out of this whole structure of the human body, every little muscle, every single cell has its own secretion and its own work. Though some physicians have said this and that organ might be spared, I believe that there is not a single thread in the whole embroidery of human nature that could well be spared—the whole of the fabric is required. So in the mystical body, the church, the least member is necessary, the most uncomely member of the Christian church is needful for its growth. Find out, then, what your sphere is and occupy it. Ask God to tell you what is your niche, and stand in it, occupying the place until Jesus Christ shall come and give you your reward. Use what ability you have and use it at once.

Andrew proved his wisdom in that *he set great store by a single soul.* He bent all his efforts at first upon one man. Afterward, Andrew, through the Holy Spirit, was made useful to scores, but he began with one. What a task for the arithmetician to value one soul! One soul sets all heaven's bells ringing by its repentance. One sinner that repents makes angels rejoice. What if you spend a whole life pleading and laboring for the conversion of that one child? If you win that pearl it shall pay you your life's worth. Be not therefore dull and discouraged because your class declines in numbers or because the mass of those with whom you labor reject your testimony. If a man could earn but one in a day he might be satisfied. "One what?" says one. I meant not one penny but one thousand pounds. "Ah," says you, "that would be an immense reward." So if you earn but one soul you must reckon what that one is. It is one for numeration, but for value it exceeds all that earth could show. What would it profit a man if he gained the whole world and lost his soul? And what loss would it be to you, dear brother or sister, if you did lose all the world and gained your soul, and God made you useful in the gaining of the souls of others? Be content and labor in your sphere, even if it be small, and you will be wise.

You may imitate Andrew in *not going far afield to do good.* Many

Christians do all the good they can five miles off from their own houses, when the time they take to go there and back might be well spent in the vineyard at home. I do not think it would be a wise regulation of the parochial authorities if they required the inhabitants of St. Mary, Newington, to remove the snow from the pavement of St. Pancras and the inhabitants of St. Pancras to keep clean the pavement of St. Mary, Newington. It is best and most convenient that each householder should sweep before his own door. So it is our duty to do, as believers, all the good we can in the place where God has been pleased to locate us and especially in our own households. If every man has a claim upon me, much more my own offspring. If every woman has some demand upon me as to her soul, so far as my ability goes, much more such as are of my own flesh and blood. Piety must begin at home as well as charity. Conversion should begin with those who are nearest to us in ties of relationship. Brethren and sisters, during this month I stir you up not to be attempting missionary labors for India, not to be casting eyes of pity across to Africa, not to be occupied so much with tears for popish and heathen lands as for your own children, your own flesh and blood, your own neighbors, your own acquaintances. Lift up your cry to heaven for them, and then afterward you shall preach among the nations. Andrew goes to Cappadocia in his afterlife, but he begins with his brother. You shall labor where you please in years to come, but first of all your own household, first of all those who are under your own shadow must receive your guardian care. Be wise in this thing. Use the ability you have, and use it among those who are near at hand.

Perhaps somebody will be saying, "How did Andrew persuade Simon Peter to come to Christ?" Two or three minutes may be spent in answering that inquiry. He did so, first, by narrating his own personal experience. He said, "We have found the Messiah." What you have experienced of Christ tell to others. He did so next by intelligently explaining to him what it was he had found. He did not say he had found someone who had impressed him, but he knew not who He was. He told him he had found Messiah, that is, Christ. Be clear in your knowledge of the Gospel and your experience of it, and then tell the good news to those whose souls you seek. Andrew had power over Peter because of his own decided conviction. He did not say, "I hope I have found Christ," but, "I have found Him." He was sure of that. Get full assurance of your own salvation. There is no weapon like it. He that speaks doubtingly of what he would convince another asks that other to doubt his testimony. Be positive in your experience and your assurance, for this will help you.

Andrew had power over Peter because he put the good news before him in an earnest fashion. He did not say to him as though it were a commonplace fact, "The Messiah has come." But no, he communicated it to him as the most weighty of all messages with becoming tones and gestures, I doubt not, "We have found the Messiah, which is called Christ." Now then, brethren and sisters, to your own kinsfolk tell your belief, your enjoyments, and your assurance. Tell all judiciously, with assurance of the truth of it, and who can tell whether God may not bless your work?

His Sweet Reward

Andrew's reward was that he won a soul, won his brother's soul, won such a treasure! He won no other than that Simon who at the first cast of the Gospel net, when Christ had made him a soul fisherman, caught three thousand souls at a single haul! Peter, a very prince in the Christian church, one of the mightiest of the servants of the Lord in all his after usefulness, would be a comfort to Andrew. I should not wonder but what Andrew would say in days of doubt and fear, "Blessed be God that he has made Peter so useful. Blessed be God that ever I spoke to Peter! What I cannot do, Peter will help to do. While I sit down in my helplessness, I can feel thankful that my dear brother Peter is honored in bringing souls to Christ."

In this house today there may sit an unconverted Whitefield. In your class this afternoon there may be an unsaved John Wesley, a Calvin, or a Luther, mute and inglorious, yet who is to be called by grace through you. Your fingers are yet to wake to ecstasy the living lyre of a heart that up until now has not been tuned to the praise of Christ. You are to kindle the fire that shall light up a sacred sacrifice of a consecrated life to Christ. Only be up and doing for the Lord Jesus, be importunate and prayerful, be zealous and self-sacrificing. Unite with us, during this month, in your daily prayers. Constantly, while in business, let your hearts go up for the blessing. I make no doubt of it, that, when we have proved our God by prayer, He will pour us down such a blessing that we shall not have room to receive it. The Lord make it so, for His name's sake. Amen.

3

Nathanael and the Fig Tree

Philip findeth Nathanael, and saith unto him, We have found him, of whom Moses in the law, and the prophets, did write, Jesus of Nazareth, the son of Joseph. And Nathanael said unto him, Can there any good thing come out of Nazareth? Philip saith unto him, Come and see. Jesus saw Nathanael coming to him, and saith of him, Behold an Israelite indeed, in whom is no guile! Nathanael saith unto him, Whence knowest thou me? Jesus answered and said unto him, Before that Philip called thee, when thou wast under the fig tree, I saw thee. Nathanael answered and saith unto him, Rabbi, thou art the Son of God; thou art the King of Israel. Jesus answered and said unto him, Because I said unto thee, I saw thee under the fig tree, believest thou? thou shalt see greater things than these. And he saith unto him, Verily, verily, I say unto you, Hereafter ye shall see heaven open, and the angels of God ascending and descending upon the Son of man (John 1:45–51).

Very often we address the Gospel to the chief of sinners. We believe it to be our duty to do this with the greatest frequency. For did not our Lord, when bidding His disciples to preach the good news in every place, use the words, "beginning at Jerusalem"? Where the chief of sinners lived, there was the Gospel first to be preached. But at the same time it would show great lack of observation if we regarded all mankind as being equally gross, open offenders against God. It would not only show a want of wisdom, but it would involve a want of truthfulness. For though all have sinned and deserve the wrath of God, yet all unconverted men are not precisely in the same condition of mind in reference to the Gospel.

This sermon was taken from *The Metropolitan Tabernacle Pulpit* and was preached on Sunday morning, March 20, 1870.

In the parable of the sower, we are taught that before the good seed fell upon the field at all there was a difference in the various soils. Some of it was stony ground, another part was thorny, a third was trodden hard like a highway, while another plot is described by our Lord as honest and good ground. Although in every case the carnal mind is enmity against God, yet are there influences at work that in many cases have mitigated, if not subdued, that enmity. While many took up stones to kill our Lord, there were others who heard Him gladly. While to this day thousands reject the Gospel, there are others who receive the Word with joy. These differences we ascribe to God's prevenient grace. We believe, however, that the subject of those differences is not aware that grace is at work upon him, neither is it precisely grace in the same form as saving grace, for the soul under its power has not yet learned its own need of Christ or the excellency of His salvation.

There is such a thing as a preparatory work of mercy on the soul making it ready for the yet higher work of grace, even as the plowing comes before the sowing. We read in the narrative of the Creation that before the divine voice said, "Let there be light," darkness was upon the face of the deep. Yet it is added, "The Spirit of God moved upon the face of the waters" (see Gen. 1). Even so in the darkness of human nature where as yet no ray of living light has shone, the Spirit of God may be moving with secret energy making the soul ready for the hour when the true light shall shine. I believe that in our congregations there are many persons who have been mercifully restrained from the grosser vices and who exhibit everything that is pure and excellent in moral character, persons who are not maliciously opposed to the Gospel, who are ready enough to receive it if they did but understand it, who are even anxious to be saved by Jesus Christ, and who have a reverence for His name, though as yet it is an ignorant reverence. They know so little of the Redeemer that they are not able to find rest in Him. But this slenderness of knowledge is the only thing that holds them back from faith in Him. They are willing enough to obey if they understood the command. If they had but a clear apprehension of our Lord's person and work, they would cheerfully accept Him as their Lord and God. I have great hopes that the Lord of love may guide the word that is now to be spoken so that it may find out such persons and may make manifest the Lord's secretly chosen ones, those prisoners of hope who pine for liberty but know not that the Son can make them free. O captive soul abhorring the chains of sin, your day of liberty is come! The Lord, the liberator who loosens the prisoners, is come at this very hour to snap your bonds.

Nathanael's Character

We are told that he was *a guileless man*, "an Israelite indeed, in whom is no guile," that is to say, like Jacob, "he was a plain man," and not like Esau, "a cunning hunter." Some minds are naturally serpentine, tortuous, slippery. They cannot think except in curves. Their motives are involved and intricate, and they are of double hearts. These are the men who look one way and row the other. They worship the god Janus with two faces and are of the same practice, if not of the same persuasion, as the Jesuits. They cannot speak a thing out plainly or look you in the face while they talk, for they are full of mental reservations and prudential cautions. They guard their speech. They dare not send abroad their own thoughts until they have nailed them up to the throat with double meanings. Nathanael was just the very opposite of all this. He was no hypocrite and no crafty deceiver. He wore his heart upon his sleeve. If he spoke, you might know that he said what he meant and that he meant what he said. He was a childlike, simple-hearted man, transparent as glass. He was not one of those fools who believe everything. But on the other hand, he was not of that other sort of fools, so much admired in these days, who will believe nothing but who find it necessary to doubt the most self-evident truth in order to maintain their credit for profound philosophy. These "thinkers" of this enlightened age are great at quibbles, mighty in feigning or feeling mistrust concerning matters that common sense has no doubts about. They will profess to doubt whether there is a God, though that be as plain as the sun at noonday. No, Nathanael was neither credulous nor mistrustful. He was honestly ready to yield to the force of truth. He was willing to receive testimony and to be swayed by evidence. He was not suspicious because he was not a man who himself would be suspected. He was truehearted and straightforward—a plain dealer and plain speaker. Cana had not within her gates a more thoroughly honest man. This Philip seems to have known, for he went to him directly as to a man who was likely to be convinced and who was worth winning to the good cause.

In addition to being thus a simple-hearted man, Nathanael was *an earnest seeker*. Philip found him out because he felt that the good news would interest him. "We have found the Messiah" would be no gladsome news to anyone who had not looked for the Messiah. But Nathanael had been expecting the Christ and perhaps had so well understood Moses and the prophets that he had been led to look for His speedy coming. The time when Messiah would suddenly come in His temple had certainly arrived. He was day and night with prayer, like all the faithful of the ten tribes, watching and waiting for the appearing of their salvation. He had not as yet heard that the glory of Israel had indeed come, but he was on the tiptoe of expectation. What a hopeful state of heart is yours, my dear hearer, if you are now honestly desirous to know the truth and intensely anxious to be saved by it! It is well indeed for you if your soul is ready, like the photographer's sensitive plate, to receive the impression of the divine light, if you are anxiously desiring to be informed if there be indeed a Savior, if there be a Gospel, if there be hope for you, if there be such a thing as purity and a way to reach it. It is well, I say, if you are anxiously, earnestly desiring to know how and when and where and determinately resolved, by God's grace, that no exertion shall be spared on your part to run in the way that shall be marked out and to submit yourself to the will of God. This was the state of Nathanael, an honest-hearted lover of plain truth, seeking to find the Christ.

It is also true that he was *ignorant* up to a certain point. He was not ignorant of Moses and the prophets, these he had well considered, but he knew not that Christ as yet had come. There was some little distance between Nazareth and Cana, and the news of the Messiah's coming had not traveled thither. If it had been bad news, it would have flown on eagles' wings, but being good news, its flight was slower, for few persons are so anxious to tell out the good as the evil. He had not therefore heard of Jesus of Nazareth until Philip came to him. And how many there are even in this country who do not know yet what the Gospel means but are anxious to know it and if they did but know it would receive it! "What," say you, "where there are so many places of worship and so many ministers?" Yes, just that. Aye, and in the very heart of our congregations and in the midst of our godly families, ignorance has its strongholds. These uninstructed ones may be Bible readers, they may be Gospel hearers, but as yet they may not have been able to grasp the great truth that God was in Christ reconciling the world to Himself. They may never have seen what it is for Christ to stand in the sinner's place and for that sinner by an act of trust to obtain the blessings that spring out of a substitutionary sacrifice. Yes, and here in this house where I have tried and labored to put the Gospel in short Saxon words and sentences that cannot be misunderstood, there may be some who are still saying, "What is this all about? I hear much of believing, but what is it? Who is this Christ, the Son of God, and what is it to be saved from sin, to be regenerated, to be sanctified? What are all these things?" Well, dear friends, I am sorry you should be in the dark, yet am I glad at heart that though you do not know what I would have you know, yet you are simple-hearted, truth-loving, and sincere in your seeking. I am persuaded that light will not be denied you; you shall yet know Jesus and be known of Him.

In addition to this, however, Nathanael was *prejudiced*—we must modify that expression—he was somewhat prejudiced. As soon as Philip told him that he had found Jesus of Nazareth, the son of Joseph, Nathanael said, "Can any good thing come out of Nazareth?" Here let us remark that his prejudice is exceedingly excusable, for it arose out of the faulty testimony of Philip. Philip was a young convert. He had only found Jesus the day before, and the natural instinct of every truly gracious soul is to try and tell out the blessed things of Christ. So away went Philip to tell his friend Nathanael, but what a many blunders he made in the telling out the Gospel! I bless God, blundering as it was, it was enough to bring Nathanael to Christ, but it was full of mistakes. Dear souls, if you know only a little about Christ and if you would make a great many mistakes in telling out that little, yet do not hold it in. God will overlook the errors and bless the truth.

Now observe what Philip said. He said, "We have found Jesus of Nazareth, the son of Joseph," which was our Lord's popular name but was in no way correct. He was not Jesus *of Nazareth* at all. He was not a native of Nazareth; our Lord was of Bethlehem. He had dwelt at Nazareth certainly, but he was no more entitled to be called of Nazareth than of Jerusalem. Then Philip said, "son of Joseph," but He was only the reputed son of Joseph. He was, in truth, the Son of the Highest. Philip gave to our Lord the common and erroneous titles that the unthinking many passed from hand to hand. He did not say, We have found the Son of God, or the Son of David, yet he uttered all he knew, and that is all God expects of you or me. Oh, what a mercy it is that the imperfections of our ministries do not prevent God's saving souls by us! If it were not so, how little good would be done in the world!

Mr. John Wesley preached most earnestly one view of the Gospel, and William Huntingdon preached quite another view of it. The two men would have had a holy horror of each other and censured each other most conscientiously. Yet no rational man dare say that souls were not saved under John Wesley or under William Huntingdon either, for God blessed them both. Both ministers were faulty, but both were sincere and both made useful. So is it with all our testimonies. They are all imperfect, full of exaggerations of one truth and misapprehensions of another. But as long as we witness to the true Christ foretold by Moses and the prophets, our mistakes shall be forgiven, and God will bless our ministries, despite every flaw.

So He did with Nathanael, but Nathanael's prejudice rose out of Philip's blundering way of talking. If Philip had not said "of Nazareth," then Nathanael would not have said, "Can any good thing come out of Nazareth?" If Philip had said that Jesus was of Bethlehem of the tribe of Judah and that God was His Father, then this prejudice would never

have beclouded the mind of Nathanael. It would have been easier for
him to have acknowledged Jesus as the Messiah. We must, therefore,
try to avoid mistakes, lest we cause needless prejudice. We should so
state the Gospel that if men be offended by it, it shall be the Gospel that
offends them and not our way of putting it. It may be that you, my
friend, are a little prejudiced against Christ's holy Gospel because of
the imperfect character of a religious acquaintance or the rough manners of a certain minister, but I trust you will not allow such things to
bias you. I hope that you, being candid and honest, will come and see
Jesus for yourself. Revise the report of the disciple by a personal in-
spection of the Master. Philip made up for his faults when he added,
"Come and see." And I would try to prevent mine from injuring you by
using the same exhortation. Come and see Jesus and His Gospel for
yourself.

One other mark of Nathanael I would mention: he was in all respects
a godly, sincere man, up to the measure of his light. He was not yet a
believer in Jesus, but still he was an Israelite indeed. He was a man of
secret prayer. He did not mock God as the Pharisees did by mere
outward worship. He was a worshiper of God in his heart. His soul had
private dealings with the God of heaven when no eye saw him. So it is,
I trust, with you, dear hearer, you may not yet have found peace, but
you do pray. You are desirous of being saved. You do not wish to be a
hypocrite. You dread, above all things, falling into formality. You pray
that if ever you become a Christian you may be a Christian indeed.
Such is the character I am endeavoring to find out, and if it is your
character, may you get the blessing that Nathanael did.

Nathanael's Sight of Jesus

"Philip saith unto him, Come and see." So Nathanael came to see the
Savior, which implies that although he was somewhat prejudiced
against this new Messiah, yet he was candid enough to investigate His
claims. Beloved friend, of whom I have already spoken, if you have any
prejudice against the true Gospel of Jesus Christ, whether it be occasioned by your birth and education or previous profession of some
other faith, be honest enough to give the Gospel of Jesus Christ a fair
hearing. You may hear it in this house; you may read it in these pages.
Do not dismiss it until you have thoroughly examined it. All that we
would ask of you is now, knowing you to be honest, knowing you to be
earnest, seriously to sit down and weigh the doctrines of grace as you
shall find them in the Scripture and especially the life of Christ and the
blessings that He brings to those who believe in Him. Look these things
over carefully; they will commend themselves to your conscience, for
God has already prepared your conscience to judge righteously. As you

judge, you will perceive a peculiar beauty and a charm about the truths of the Gospel that will surely win your heart. Latimer had preached a sermon against the doctrines of the Gospel. Among his hearers there was a holy man, who afterward became a martyr, who thought as he listened to Latimer that he perceived something in his tone that showed him to be an honest opponent. Therefore, he hoped that if light were brought to him he would be willing to see by it. He sought him out, obtained an interview with him, and his explanations entirely won honest Hugh to the Reformed opinions. And you know what a valiant and popular minister of the new covenant he became. So, my honest friend, give to the Gospel of salvation by faith in the precious blood of Jesus a fair hearing, and we are not afraid of the result.

Nathanael came to Christ with *great activity* of heart. As soon as he was told to "come and see," he did come and see. He did not sit still and say, "Well, if there is any light in this new doctrine, it will come to me," but he went to it. Do not believe in any teaching that bids men sit down and find peace in the idea that they need not strive to enter in at the strait gate of truth. No, friends, if grace has ever come to you, it will arouse you from lethargy and lead you to go to Christ. You will be most earnest with all the activity of your spirit to search for Him as for hid treasure. It is a delightful thing to see a soul on the wing. The mass of our population are, as regards to religion, down on the ground and unwilling to rise. They are indifferent to spiritual truth. You cannot get them to give earnest heed to eternal matters. But once you get a mind on the wing with a holy earnestness and solemn thoughtfulness, we do believe that, with God's grace, it will before long be brought to a saving faith in Christ. "Come and see," said Philip, and come and see Nathanael did. He does not appear to have expected to be converted to Christ by what he saw with his natural eyes. His judgment was formed from a mental view of Him. It is true he saw the person of the Messiah, but he did not expect to see in the human form any lineaments that might guide his judgment. He waited until the lips of the Messiah had spoken. Then, when he had seen the omniscience of that mysterious person, and how He could read his thoughts and spy out his secret actions, then he believed.

Now, I fear some of you live in darkness because you are expecting some kind of physical manifestation. You hope for a vivid dream or some strange feeling in your flesh or some very remarkable occurrence in your family; except you see signs and wonders you will not believe. No, but a saving sight of Christ is another matter. Truth must impress your mental faculties, enlighten your understanding, and win your affections. The presence of Christ on earth is a spiritual one, and you will come to see Him not with these mortal optics just now but with the eyes of your soul. You will perceive the beauty of His character, the majesty of His person, the all sufficiency of His atonement. As you see these things the Holy Spirit will lead you to believe in Him and live. I pray God that such a sight as this may be vouchsafed to every honest seeker who may hear or read these words.

Nathanael in Jesus' Sight

As soon as Jesus saw the man, he said, "Behold an Israelite indeed," which shows us that Christ Jesus read Nathanael's heart. I do not suppose that our Lord had ever seen Nathanael with His own human eyes. Yet He understood Nathanael's character not because He was a great judge of physiognomy and could perceive at once that He had a simple-hearted man before him, but because being Nathanael's Creator, being the searcher of hearts and the trier of the reins, He could read Nathanael as readily as a man reads a book that is open before his eyes. He saw at once all that was within the inquirer and pronounced a verdict upon him that he was free from falsehood. And then to prove to Nathanael still further how clearly He knew all about him, He mentioned a little incident that I cannot explain nor can you, nor do I suppose anybody could have explained it except Nathanael and Jesus—a special secret known only to them both. He said to him, "Before that Philip called thee, when thou wast under the fig tree, I saw thee." What he was doing under the fig tree we may guess, but we cannot know to a certainty. Perhaps it would be truest of all to believe that the fig tree was to Nathanael what the Hermonites and the hill Mizar had been to David. David says, "I will remember thee from the land of Jordan, and of the Hermonites, and from the hill Mizar" (Ps. 42:6). What were those sacred recollections he does not tell us. Although we can form a shrewd guess, David and his God alone knew the full mystery. So between Christ and Nathanael there was a common knowledge connected with that fig tree that we cannot hope to discover. The moment our Lord mentioned that hallowed spot, its remembrances were to Nathanael so secret and so sacred that he felt that the omniscient One was before him. Here was evidence that he could not doubt for an instant, for one of the most private and special secrets of his life which he had never whispered into any human ear, had been brought up as by a talismanic sign. A red-letter day in his private diary had been revived by the mention of the fig tree, and He who could touch so hidden a spring in his soul must be the Son of God.

But what was Nathanael doing under the fig tree, according to our best surmise? Well, as devout Easterners are accustomed to have a special place for prayer, this may have been a shadowy fig tree under which Nathanael was accustomed to offer his devotions. Perhaps just before Philip came to him, he may have been engaged in personal and solitary *confession of sin.* He had looked around the garden and fastened the gate that none might come in. He had poured into the ear of his God some very tender confession under the fig tree's shade. When Christ said to him, "When thou wast under the fig tree," it brought to his recollection how he poured out his broken and contrite spirit and confessed sins unknown to all but God. That confession, it may be, the very look of Christ brought back to his remembrance. The words and look together seemed to say, "I know your secret burden and the peace you found in rolling it upon the Lord." He felt therefore that Jesus must be Israel's God.

It is very possible that in addition to his confession, he had under the fig tree made a *deliberate investigation of his own heart.* Good men generally mingle with their confessions self-examination. There it may be that this man who was free from guile had looked into the tendencies of his nature and had been enabled with holy surprise to see the fountains of the great deep of his natural depravity. He may have been taken, like Ezekiel, from chamber to chamber to see the idols in his heart, beholding greater abominations than he suspected to be there, and there have been humbled before the Lord. Beneath that fig tree he may have cried with Job, "I abhor myself, and repent in dust and ashes" (Job 42:6). This also Jesus had seen.

Or under the fig tree he had been engaged in *very earnest prayer.* Was that fig tree to Nathanael what Peniel was to Jacob, a spot wherein he had wrestled until the break of day, pleading with God to fulfill His ancient promise to send the promised One who should be a light to lighten the Gentiles and the glory of His people Israel? Was it so? We think it probable. That fig tree had been to him a Bethel, no other than the house of God and the very gate of heaven.

And what if we should suggest that perhaps in addition to his prayer, Nathanael had *vowed* some solemn vow under the fig tree—if the Lord would but appear and give to him some sign and token for good, then he would be the Lord's and spend and be spent for Him. If the Lord would but send the Messiah, he would be among His first followers. If He would but speak to him by an angel or otherwise, he would obey the voice. Jesus now tells him that he shall see angels ascending and descending, and reveals Himself as the Messiah to whom he had solemnly pledged himself. It may be so.

It may be that under that fig tree he had enjoyed the sweetest *communion* with his God. Beloved friends, do you not remember well certain hallowed spots? I have one or two in my own life too sacred to mention. If my memory should forget all the world besides, yet those spots will evermore be green in my memory, the truly holy place where Jesus my Lord has met with me and showed me His love. One time it was "the king hath brought me into his chambers" (Song 1:4), another time I gat me to "the mountain of myrrh, and to the hill of frankincense" (4:6). Once He said, "Come, my beloved, let us go forth into field; let us lodge in the villages" (7:11). And anon He changed the scene and said, "Come with me from Lebanon, my spouse, with me from . . . Hermon, from the lions' dens, from the mountains of the leopards" (4:8). Have we not sometimes had special festivals when He has broached the spiced wine of His pomegranate? When our joy has been almost too much for the frail body to endure, for our joyous spirits, like a sharp sword, have well-nigh cut through their scabbards? Ah, it is sweetly true, those secret spots, those dear occasions. This then was a token, a secret token between Christ and Nathanael, by which the disciple met the Messiah in spirit before. Now he meets Him in very flesh and blood, and by this token does he know Him. In spirit the Lord set His seal upon Nathanael's heart, and now by the sacred signet the Israelite indeed discerns his King.

Thus we see the Lord had seen Nathanael in his previous engagements before he became actually a believer in Jesus. This fact suggests that each of you who have been sincerely seeking to be set right and to know the truth have been fully perceived in all your seekings and desirings by the God of grace. When you let fall a tear because you could not understand the Word, Jesus saw that tear. When you groaned because you could not get satisfaction of heart, He heard that groan. Never true heart seeks Christ without Christ's being well aware of it. Well may He know of it, for every motion of a trembling heart toward Him is caused by His own love. He is drawing you, though you perceive not the bands of a man that encircle you. He is the hidden loadstone by which your heart is moved. I know it is night with you, and you grope like a blind man for the wall, but if your heart says, "O that I could but embrace Him! O that He were mine! If I could but find rest in Him, I would give all that I have," then be assured that Jesus is close to you. Your prayers are in His ears, your tears fall upon His heart. He knows all about your difficulties, all about your doubts and fears, and He sympathizes in the whole. In due time He will break your snares, and you shall yet with joy draw water out of the wells of salvation. This truth is full of consolation to all who seek with sincerity, though as yet in the dark. Before the minister's voice spoke to you, when you were under the fig tree, when you were by the bedside, when you were in that inner chamber, when you were down in that saw pit, when you were in the hayloft, when you were walking behind the hedge in the field, Jesus saw you. He knew your desires. He read your longings. He saw you through and through. Even from of old He has known you.

Nathanael's Faith

I must go over much the same ground again under this head, Nathanael's faith. Note *what it was grounded on.* He cheerfully accepted Jesus as the Messiah. The ground of his acceptance lay in this: Jesus had mentioned to him a peculiar incident in his life that he was persuaded no one could have known but the omniscient God. Thereon he concluded Jesus to be the omniscient God and accepted Him at once as his King. This was very frequently the way in which persons were brought to confidence in Christ. The same thing is recorded in this very Gospel a few chapters further on. The Lord sat down on the well and talked to the Samaritan woman, and there was no kind of impression produced upon her until He said, "Thou hast had five husbands; and he whom thou now hast is not thine husband" (John 4:18). Then it flashed upon her, "This stranger knows my private history! Then He is something more than He appears to be. He is the Great Prophet." Away she ran with this on her tongue because it was in her heart, "Come, see a man, which told me all things that ever I did: is not this the Christ?" (v. 29). The same was the case with Zacchaeus. You may perhaps think, however, that this mode of conversion was confined to the days of our Lord's flesh and to the age of miracles, but it is not so. The fact is that at this very day the discovery of the thoughts of men's hearts by the Gospel is still a very potent means in the hands of the Holy Spirit of convincing them of the truth of the Gospel. How often have I heard inquirers say, "It seemed to me, sir, as if that sermon was meant for me. There were points in it that were so exactly like me that I felt sure someone had told the preacher about me. There were words and sentences so peculiarly descriptive of my private thought that I was sure no one but God knew of them. I perceived that God was in the Gospel speaking to my soul." Yes, and it always will be so. The Gospel is the great revealer of secrets. It is a discerner of the thoughts and intents of the heart. Jesus Christ in the Gospel knows all about your sin, all about your seeking, all about the difficulties that you are meeting with. This ought to convince you that the Gospel is divine, since its teachings lay bare the heart, and its remedies touch every spiritual disease. The knowledge of human nature displayed in the simplest passage of the Gospel is more profound than the productions of Plato or Socrates. The Gospel, like a silken clue, runs through all the windings and twistings of human nature in its fallen state. O that its voice may come home personally so to you. May it by the Spirit convince you of sin, of righteousness, and of judgment and bring you to lay hold on eternal life.

Nathanael's faith, it must be mentioned, was peculiar not only in its ground, but *in its clear and comprehensive character.* He accepted

Jesus at once as the Son of God. He was divine to him, and he adored Him. He also accepted Him as the King of Israel. He was a royal personage to him, and he tendered Him his homage. May you and I receive Jesus Christ in this way, as a real man, yet certainly God. He was the man who was despised and rejected yet the man anointed above His brethren, who is King of Kings and Lord of Lords.

I admire Nathanael's faith because it was so *quick, unreserved, and decisive*. "Thou art the Son of God; thou art the King of Israel." Christ was glorified by the decision, the quickness of this faith. Delay in believing Him dishonors Him. O honest heart, O sincere mind, pray that you may as quickly come into the light and liberty of true belief. May the Holy Spirit work in you a ready satisfaction in the atoning sacrifice and divine person of the ever blessed Immanuel.

Nathanael's Sight Afterward

Some persons want to see all that there is in Christianity before they can believe in Jesus. That is to say, before they will go to the dame school they must needs clamor for a degree at the university. Many want to know the ninth of Romans before they have read the third of John. They are all for understanding great mysteries before they understand that primary simplicity, Believe and live. But those who are wiser and, like Nathanael, are content to believe at first what they are able to perceive, namely, that Christ is the Son of God and the King of Israel, shall go on to learn more. Let us read our Lord's words, "Thou shalt see greater things than these. . . . Verily, verily, I say unto you, Hereafter ye shall see heaven open, and the angels of God ascending and descending upon the Son of man" (1:50–51). To full-grown disciples Jesus promises, "Greater things than these shall [ye] do" (John 14:12); to young converts He says, "Thou shalt see greater things than these" (1:50). He gives promises in proportion to our ability to receive them.

The promise given to Nathanael was a most fitting one. He was an Israelite indeed—thus he shall have Israel's vision. What was the great sight that Israel, or Jacob, saw? He saw the ladder whereon angels ascended and descended. Precisely this shall Nathanael see. He shall see Jesus Christ as the communication between an opened heaven and a blessed earth. He shall see the angels ascending and descending upon the Son of Man. If you bear the character of Israel, you shall enjoy the privileges of Israel. If you are an Israelite indeed, you shall have the blessing that made Israel glad. Nathanael had owned Jesus as the Son of God. Here he is told that he shall see Him in His glory as the Son of Man. Note that last word of the chapter. It is not so much that Christ humbly called Himself the Son of Man—though that is true—as this, that to see the glory of Christ as God is a simple thing. But to see and understand the glory of Christ as man, this is a sight for faith and probably a sight which, so far as our senses are concerned, is reserved for the day of His coming. When He shall appear, the very Man that suffered upon Calvary, upon the Great White Throne to judge the quick and the dead, if you believe in Jesus as the Son of God, you shall yet see Him in His glory as man swaying the universal scepter and enthroned as King of all the earth.

He had called Jesus the King of Israel, if you remember; now he is to see his Lord as the King of the angels, to see the angels of God ascending and descending upon Him. Believe, my dear brother in Christ, as far as you know Him, and you shall know more of Him. Open your eyes but to the candlelight of the law, and you shall soon behold the sunlight of the Gospel. The Lord is very gracious to fulfill the Gospel rule, "Unto everyone that hath shall be given, and he shall have abundance" (Matt. 25:29). If you do acknowledge the King of Israel, you shall see Him as the Lord of Hosts before whom archangels veil their faces, and to whom seraphim are servitors.

The great sight, I suppose, Nathanael did see as the result of his faith was not the transfiguration nor the ascension, as some suppose, but a spiritual view of Christ in His mediatorial capacity as the great link between earth and heaven. This is indeed a sight transcending all others. We are not divided from the invisible, we are not separated from the infinite, the mortal has communion with immortal, the sinner speaks with the Holy One, prayers climb up to heaven, and benisons descend by way of the Great Substitute. Can you see this, O soul? If so, the sight will make you glad. You are not exiled now, you are only at the foot of the stairs that lead to the upper chamber of your Father's house. Your God is above and bright spirits traverse constantly the open gangway of the Mediator's person. Here is joy for all the saints, for this ladder can never be broken. Our communion is abiding.

No doubt, to Nathanael's view, the promise would be fulfilled as he perceived the providence of God as ruled by Christ Jesus, who orders all things for the good of the church. Was not this intended in the figure of angels ascending and descending upon the Son of Man, that is, all agencies whether living or material, all subject to the law and the dominion of Christ—so that all things work together for good to them that love God? Do not go fretting to your homes and say, "Here are new doctrines springing up and new gods that our fathers knew not. Ministers are slipping aside from the faith, and bad days have fallen upon the church. Romanism is coming up, and infidelity with it." All this may be true, but it does not matter one fig for the great end that God has in view. He has a bit for the mouth of leviathan. He can do as He wills with His most powerful enemies. He rides upon the wings of cherubs and rules the storm. The clouds are but the dust of His feet.

Believe never that providence is out of joint. The wheels of this great engine may revolve some this way and some that, but the sure result will be produced, for the great Artist sees the final result to be secure. God's glory shall arise from it all. Angels descend, but they as much do the will of God as those that ascend. Some events seem disastrous and even calamitous. But they shall all, in the end, prove to be for the best; for He

> From seeming evil still enduceth good,
> And better still, and better still, in infinite progression.

Until the crown shall come upon the head of Him who was separated from His brethren and sisters, and all the glory shall roll in waves of mighty song at the foot of His throne, may you and I continue to see this great sight more and more clearly. Until the Lord shall descend from heaven with a shout, with the trump of the archangel, and the voice of God, and once for all shall we see heaven and earth blended, may we continue to see angels ascending and descending upon the Son of Man. All this matchless glory will come to us through that little window by which we first saw the Savior. If we will not see Him as our Lord until we can see all the future, we shall perish in darkness. If you will not believe, neither shall you be established. But if, with simple and true hearts, you have been seeking Jesus, and now come and accept Him as the Lord, the King of Israel, then greater things than these shall be in store for you. Your eyes shall see the King in His beauty and the land that is very far off and the day of His pompous appearing, when heaven and earth shall hang out their streamers for overflowing joy because the King has come to His own and the crown is put upon the head of the Son of David. Then shall you see it and see it all, for you shall be with Him where He is that you may behold His glory—the glory that the Father gave Him before the foundation of the world.

4

The Dying Thief in a New Light

But the other answering rebuked him, saying, Dost not thou fear God, seeing thou art in the same condemnation? And we indeed justly; for we receive the due reward of our deeds: but this man hath done nothing amiss. And he said unto Jesus, Lord, remember me when thou comest into thy kingdom (Luke 23:40–42).

A great many persons, whenever they hear of the conversion of the dying thief, remember that he was saved in the very article of death, and they dwell upon that fact and that alone. He has always been quoted as a case of salvation at the eleventh hour, and so, indeed, he is. In his case it is proven that as long as a man can repent he can obtain forgiveness. The cross of Christ avails even for a man hanging on a gibbet and drawing near to his last hour. He who is mighty to save was mighty, even during His own death, to pluck others from the grasp of the destroyer, though they were in the act of expiring.

But that is not everything that the story teaches us. It is always a pity to look exclusively upon one point and thus to miss everything else— perhaps miss that which is more important. So often has this been the case that it has produced a sort of revulsion of feeling in certain minds so that they have been driven in a wrong direction by their wish to protest against what they think to be a common error. I read the other day that this story of the dying thief ought not to be taken as an encouragement to deathbed repentance. Brethren and sisters, if the author meant—and I do not think he did mean—that this ought never to be so used as to lead people to postpone repentance to a dying bed, he spoke correctly. No Christian man could or would use it so injuriously.

This sermon was taken from *The Metropolitan Tabernacle Pulpit* and was preached on Sunday evening, August 23, 1885.

He must be hopelessly bad who would draw from God's long-suffering an argument for continuing in sin. I trust, however, that the narrative is not often so used even by the worst of men, and I feel sure that it will not be so used by any one of you. It cannot be properly turned to such a purpose. It might be used as an encouragement to thieving just as much as to the delay of repentance. I might say, "I may be a thief because this thief was saved," just as rationally as I might say, "I may put off repentance because this thief was saved when he was about to die." The fact is there is nothing so good but men can pervert it into evil if they have evil hearts. The justice of God is made a motive for despair and His mercy an argument for sin. Wicked men will drown themselves in the rivers of truth as readily as in the pools of error. He that has a mind to destroy himself can choke his soul with the Bread of Life or dash himself in pieces against the Rock of Ages. There is no doctrine of the grace of God so gracious that graceless men may not turn it into licentiousness.

I venture, however, to say that if I stood by the bedside of a dying man tonight and found him anxious about his soul but fearful that Christ could not save him because repentance had been put off so late, I would certainly quote the dying thief to him. I would do it with good conscience and without hesitation. I would tell him that, though he was as near to dying as the thief upon the cross was, yet, if he repented of his sin and turned his face to Christ believingly, he would find eternal life. I would do this with all my heart, rejoicing that I had such a story to tell to one at the gates of eternity. I do not think that I should be censured by the Holy Spirit for thus using a narrative that He has Himself recorded—recorded with the foresight that it would be so used. I would feel, at any rate, in my own heart a sweet conviction that I had treated the subject as I ought to have treated it and as it was intended to be used for men *in extremis* whose hearts are turning toward the living God. Oh, yes, poor soul, whatever your age or whatever the period of life to which you have come, you may now find eternal life by faith in Christ!

> The dying thief rejoiced to see
> That fountain in his day;
> And there may you, though vile as he,
> Wash all your sins away.

Many good people think that they ought to guard the Gospel. But it is never so safe as when it stands out in its own naked majesty. It wants no covering from us. When we protect it with provisos and guard it with exceptions and qualify it with observations, it is like David in Saul's armor. It is hampered and hindered, and you may even hear it cry, "I cannot go with these." Let the Gospel alone, and it will save.

Qualify it and the salt has lost its savor. I will venture to put it thus to you. I have heard it said that few are ever converted in old age. This is thought to be a statement that will prove exceedingly arousing and impressive for the young. It certainly wears that appearance. But, on the other hand, it is a statement very discouraging to the old. I demur to the frequent repetition of such statements, for I do not find their counterpart in the teaching of our Lord and His apostles. Assuredly our Lord spoke of some who entered the vineyard at the eleventh hour of the day. Among His miracles He not only saved those who were dying, but even raised the dead. Nothing, from the words of the Lord Jesus, can be concluded against the salvation of men at any hour or age. I tell you that in the business of your acceptance with God through faith in Christ Jesus, it does not matter what age you now are at. The same promise is to every one of you, "To day if ye will hear his voice, harden not your hearts" (Heb. 4:7). Whether you are in the earliest stage of life or are within a few hours of eternity, if now you fly for refuge to the hope set before you in the Gospel, you shall be saved. The Gospel that I preach excludes none on the ground either of age or of character. Whoever you may be, "Believe on the Lord Jesus Christ, and thou shalt be saved" (Acts 16:31) is the message we have to deliver to you. If we address to you the longer form of the Gospel, "He that believeth and is baptized shall be saved" (Mark 16:16) this is true of every living man, be his age whatever it may. I am not afraid that this story of the dying and repenting thief, who went straight from the cross to the crown, will be used by you amiss. But if you are wicked enough so to use it, I cannot help it. It will only fulfill that solemn Scripture which says that the Gospel is a savor of death to death to some, even that very Gospel which is a savor of life to life to others.

But I do not think, dear friends, that the only specialty about the thief is the lateness of his repentance. So far from being the only point of interest, it is not even the chief point. To some minds, at any rate, other points will be even more remarkable. I want to show you very briefly that there was a specialty in his case as to *the means of his conversion*; secondly, a specialty in *his faith*; thirdly, a specialty in *the result of his faith* while he was here below; and, fourthly, a specialty in *the promise won by his faith*—the promise fulfilled to him in paradise.

The Specialty of the
Means of This Man's Conversion

How do you think it was that this man was converted? Well, we do not know. We cannot tell. It seems to me that the man was an unconverted, impenitent thief when they nailed him to the cross, because one of the Evangelists says, "The thieves also, which were crucified with him, cast the same in his teeth" (Matt. 27:44). I know that this may have been a general statement and that it is reconcilable with its having been done by one thief only, according to the methods commonly used by critics. But I am not enamored of critics even when they are friendly. I have such respect for revelation that I never in my own mind permit the idea of discrepancies and mistakes. When the Evangelist says "they" I believe he meant *they* and that both these thieves did at their first crucifixion rail at the Christ with whom they were crucified. It would appear that by some means or other this thief must have been converted while he was on the cross. Assuredly nobody preached a sermon to him, no evangelistic address was delivered at the foot of his cross, and no meeting was held for special prayer on his account. He does not even seem to have had an instruction or an invitation or an expostulation addressed to him; yet this man became a sincere and accepted believer in the Lord Jesus Christ.

Dwell upon this fact, if you please, and note its practical bearing upon the cases of many around us. There are many among my hearers who have been instructed from their childhood, who have been admonished, warned, entreated, and invited, yet they have not come to Christ, while this man, without any of these advantages, nevertheless believed in the Lord Jesus Christ and found eternal life. O you that have lived under the sound of the Gospel from your childhood, the thief does not comfort you, but he accuses you! What are you doing to abide so long in unbelief? Will you never believe the testimony of divine love? What more shall I say to you? What more can anyone say to you?

What do you think must have converted this poor thief? It strikes me that it may have been—it must have been, the sight of our great Lord and Savior. There was, to begin with, our Savior's wonderful behavior on the road to the cross. Perhaps the robber had mixed up with all sorts of society, but he had never seen a Man like this. Never had cross been carried by a Crossbearer of His look and fashion. The robber wondered who this meek and majestic personage could be. He heard the women weep, and he wondered in himself whether anybody would ever weep for him. He thought that this must be some very singular person that the people should stand about Him with tears in their eyes. When he heard that mysterious sufferer say so solemnly, "Daughters of Jerusalem, weep not for me, but . . . for your children" (Luke 23:28), he must have been struck with wonder. When he came to think, in his death pangs, of the singular look of pity that Jesus cast on the women and of the self-forgetfulness that gleamed from His eyes, he was smitten with a strange relenting. It was as if an angel had crossed his path and opened his eyes to a new world and to a new form of manhood the like of which he had never seen before. He and his companion were coarse, rough fellows.

This was a delicately formed and fashioned Being of superior order to him—yes, and of superior order to any other of the sons of men. Who could He be? What must He be? Though he could see that He suffered and fainted as He went along, he marked that there was no word of complaining, no note of execration in return for the revilings cast upon Him. His eyes looked love on those who glared on Him with hate. Surely that march along the Via Dolorosa was the first part of the sermon that God preached to that bad man's heart. It was preached to many others who did not regard its teaching, but upon this man, by God's special grace, it had a softening effect when he came to think over it and consider it. Was it not a likely and convincing means of grace?

When he saw the Savior surrounded by the Roman soldiery—saw the executioners bring forth the hammers and the nails and lay Him down upon His back and drive the nails into His hands and feet, this crucified criminal was startled and astonished as he heard Him say, "Father, forgive them; for they know not what they do" (Luke 23:34). He himself, probably, had met his executioners with a curse, but he heard this man breathe a prayer to the great Father. As a Jew, as he probably was, he understood what was meant by such a prayer. But it did astound him to hear Jesus pray for His murderers. That was a petition the like of which he had never heard nor even dreamed of. From whose lips could it come but from the lips of a divine Being? Such a loving, forgiving, Godlike prayer proved Him to be the Messiah. Who else had ever prayed so? Certainly not David and the kings of Israel, who, on the contrary, in all honesty and heartiness imprecated the wrath of God upon their enemies. Elias himself would not have prayed in that fashion, rather would he have called fire from heaven on the centurion and his company. It was a new, strange sound to him. I do not suppose that he appreciated it to the full. But I can well believe that it deeply impressed him and made him feel that his fellow sufferer was a Being about whom there was an exceeding mystery of goodness.

And when the cross was lifted up, that thief hanging upon his own cross looked around, and I suppose he could see that inscription written in three languages—"JESUS OF NAZARETH THE KING OF THE JEWS" (John 19:19). If so, that writing was his little Bible, his New Testament, and he interpreted it by what he knew of the Old Testament. Putting this and that together—that strange person, incarnate loveliness, all patience and all majesty, that strange prayer, and now this singular inscription—surely he who knew the Old Testament, as I have no doubt he did, would say to himself, "Is this He? Is this truly the King of the Jews? This is He who wrought miracles, raised the dead, and said that He was the Son of God. Is it all true and is He really our Messiah?"

Then he would remember the words of the prophet Isaiah, "He is despised and rejected of men; a man of sorrows, and acquainted with grief. . . . Surely he hath borne our griefs, and carried our sorrows." Why, he would say to himself, I never understood that passage in the prophet Esaias before, but it must point to Him. The chastisement of our peace is upon Him. Can this be He who cried in the Psalms, They pierced my hands and my feet? As he looked at Him again, he felt in his soul, "It must be He. Could there be another so like to Him?" He felt conviction creeping over his spirit. Then he looked again, and he marked how all men down below rejected and despised and hissed at Him and hooted Him, and all this would make the case the more clear. "All they that see me laugh me to scorn: they shoot out the lip, they shake the head, saying, He trusted on the LORD that he would deliver him: let him deliver him, seeing he delighted in him."

Peradventure, this dying thief read the Gospel out of the lips of Christ's enemies. They said, "He saved others." Ah! thought he, did he save others? Why should He not save me? What a grand bit of Gospel that was for the dying thief—"He saved others" (Luke 23:35)! I think I could swim to heaven on that plank—He saved others—because if He saved others, He can of a surety save me.

Thus the very things that the enemies disdainfully threw at Christ would be Gospel to this poor dying man. When it has been my misery to read any of the wretched prints that are sent us, out of scorn, in which our Lord is held up to ridicule, I have thought, "Why, perhaps those who read these loathsome blasphemies may, nevertheless, learn the Gospel from them!" You may pick a jewel from a dunghill and find its radiance undiminished. You may gather the Gospel from a blasphemous mouth, and it shall be nonetheless the Gospel of salvation. Peradventure this man learned the Gospel from those who jested at our dying Lord; so the servants of the Devil were unconsciously made to be the servants of Christ.

But, after all, surely that which won him most must have been to look at Jesus again as He was hanging upon the cruel tree. Possibly nothing about the physical person of Christ would be attractive to him, for His visage was more marred than that of any man and His form more than the sons of men. But there must have been in that blessed face a singular charm. Was it not the very image of perfection? As I conceive the face of Christ, it was very different from anything that any painter has yet been able to place upon his canvas. It was all goodness, kindness, and unselfishness, yet it was a royal face. It was a face of superlative justice and unrivaled tenderness. Righteousness and uprightness sat upon his brow, but infinite pity and good will to men had also there taken up their abode. It was a face that would have struck you at once as one by itself, never to be forgotten, never to be fully understood. It was all sorrow yet all love, all meekness yet all resolution, all wisdom yet all simplicity; the face of a child or an angel and yet peculiarly the face of a man. Majesty and misery, suffering and sacredness were therein strangely combined. He was evidently the Lamb of God and the Son of Man. As the robber looked, he believed. Is it not singular, the very sight of the Master won him? The sight of the Lord in agony and shame and death! Scarcely a word, certainly no sermon, no attending worship on the Sabbath, no reading of gracious books, no appeal from mother or teacher or friend, but the sight of Jesus won him. I put it down as a very singular thing, a thing for you and for me to recollect and dwell upon, with quite as much vividness as we do upon the lateness of this robber's conversion.

Oh, that God of His mercy might convert everybody in this Tabernacle! Oh, that I could have a share in it by the preaching of the Word! But I will be equally happy if you get to heaven anyhow, aye, if the Lord should take you there without outward ministries, leading you to Jesus by some simple method such as He adopted with this thief. If you do but get there, He shall have the glory of it, and His poor servant will be overjoyed! Oh, that you would now look to Jesus and live! Before your eyes He is set forth, evidently crucified among you. Look to Him and be saved, even at this hour.

The Specialty of This Man's Faith

I think it was a very singular faith that this man exerted toward our Lord Jesus Christ. I greatly question whether the equal and the parallel of the dying thief's faith will be readily found outside the Scriptures or even in the Scriptures.

Observe, that *this man believed in Christ when he saw Him literally dying the death of a felon,* under circumstances of the greatest personal shame. You have never realized what it was to be crucified. None of you could do that, for the sight has never been seen in our day in England. There is not a man or woman here who has ever realized in his or her own mind the actual death of Christ. It stands beyond us. This man saw it with his own eyes, and for him to call *Him* "Lord" who was hanging on a gibbet was no small triumph of faith. For him to ask Jesus to remember him when He came into His kingdom, though he saw that Jesus bleeding His life away and hounded to the death, was a splendid act of reliance. For him to commit his everlasting destiny into the hands of One who was, to all appearance, unable even to preserve His own life was a noble achievement of faith. I say that this dying thief leads the van in the matter of faith, for what he saw of the circumstances of the Savior was calculated to contradict rather than to help his confidence. What he saw was to his hindrance rather than to his help, for he saw our Lord in the very extremity of agony and death. Yet he believed in Him as the King shortly to come into His kingdom.

Recollect, too, that *at that moment when the thief believed in Christ, all the disciples had forsaken Him and fled*. John might be lingering at a little distance and holy women may have stood farther off, but no one was present bravely to champion the dying Christ. Judas had sold Him, Peter had denied Him, and the rest had forsaken Him. It was then that the dying thief called Him "Lord," and said, "Remember me when thou comest into thy kingdom." I call that splendid faith. Why, some of you do not believe, though you are surrounded with Christian friends— though you are urged on by the testimony of those whom you regard with love. But this man, all alone, comes out and calls Jesus his Lord! No one else was confessing Christ at that moment. No revival was around him with enthusiastic crowds. He was all by himself as a confessor of his Lord. After our Lord was nailed to the tree, the first to bear witness for Him was this thief. The centurion bore witness afterward when our Lord expired. But this thief was a lone confessor, holding on to Christ when nobody would say "Amen" to what he said. Even his fellow thief was mocking at the crucified Savior, so that this man shone as a lone star in the midnight darkness. O sirs, dare you be Daniels? Dare you stand alone? Would you dare to stand out amidst a ribald crew and say, "Jesus is my King. I only ask Him to remember me when He comes into His kingdom"? Would you be likely to avow such a faith when priests and scribes, princes and people, were all mocking at the Christ and deriding Him? Brethren, the dying robber exhibited marvelous faith, and I beg you to think of this next time you speak of Him.

And it seems to me that another point adds splendor to that faith, namely, that *he himself was in extreme torture*. Remember, he was crucified. It was a crucified man trusting in a crucified Christ. Oh, when your frame is racked with torture, when the most tender nerves are pained, when your body is hung up to die by you know not what great length of torment, then to forget the present and live in the future is a grand achievement of faith. While dying, to turn your eye to Another dying at your side and trust your soul with Him is very marvelous faith. Blessed thief, because they put you down at the bottom as one of the least of saints, I think that I must bid you come up higher and take one of the uppermost seats among those who by faith have glorified the Christ of God!

Why, see, dear friends, once more, the specialty of this man's faith was that *he saw so much*, though his eyes had been opened for so short a time! He saw the future world. He was not a believer in annihilation or in the possibility of a man's not being immortal. He evidently expected to be in another world and to be in existence when the dying Lord should come into His kingdom. He believed all that, and it is more than some do nowadays. He also believed that Jesus would have a kingdom, a kingdom after He was dead, a kingdom though He was crucified. He believed that He was winning for Himself a kingdom by those nailed hands and pierced feet. This was intelligent faith, was it not? He believed that Jesus would have a kingdom in which others would share, and therefore he aspired to have his portion in it. But he had fit views of himself, and therefore he did not say, "Lord, let me sit at Your right hand," or "Let me share of the dainties of Your palace." But he said only, "Remember me. Think of me. Cast an eye my way. Think of Your poor dying comrade on the cross at Your right hand. Lord, remember me. Remember me." I see deep humility in the prayer and yet a sweet, joyous, confident exaltation of the Christ at the time when the Christ was in His deepest humiliation.

Oh, dear people, if any of you have thought of this dying thief only as one who put off repentance, I want you now to think of him as one that did greatly and grandly believe in Christ. Oh, that you would do the same! Oh, that you would put a great confidence in my great Lord! Never did a poor sinner trust Christ too much. There was never a case of a guilty one who believed that Jesus could forgive him and afterward found that He could not—who believed that Jesus could save him on the spot and then woke up to find that it was a delusion. No; plunge into this river of confidence in Christ. The waters are waters to swim in not to drown in. Never did a soul perish that glorified Christ by a living, loving faith in Him. Come, then, with all your sin, whatever it may be, with all your deep depression of spirit, with all your agony of conscience. Come along with you, and grasp my Lord and Master with both the hands of your faith, and He shall be yours, and you shall be His.

> Turn to Christ your longing eyes,
> View His bloody sacrifice:
> See in Him your sins forgiven;
> Pardon, holiness, and heaven;
> Glorify the King of kings,
> Take the peace the Gospel brings.

I think that I have shown you something special in the means of the thief's conversion and in his faith in our dying Lord.

The Result of This Man's Faith

Oh, I have heard people say, "Well, you see, the dying thief was converted. But then he was not baptized. He never went to communion and never joined the church!" He could not do either and that which God

Himself renders impossible to us He does not demand of us. He was nailed to the cross. How could he be baptized? But he did a great deal more than that. If he could not carry out the outward signs, he most manifestly exhibited the things that they signified, which, in his condition, was better still.

This dying thief first of all confessed the Lord Jesus Christ. That is the very essence of baptism. He confessed Christ. Did he not acknowledge Him to his fellow thief? It was as open a confession as he could make it. Did he not acknowledge Christ before all that were gathered around the cross who were within hearing? It was as public a confession as he could possibly cause it to be. Yet certain cowardly fellows claim to be Christians, though they have never confessed Christ to a single person, and then they quote this poor thief as an excuse. Are they nailed to a cross? Are they dying in agony? Oh, no! Yet they talk as if they could claim the exemption that these circumstances would give them. What a dishonest piece of business!

The fact is that our Lord requires an open confession as well as a secret faith. If you will not render it, there is no promise of salvation for you but a threat of being denied at the last. The apostle puts it, "If thou shalt confess with thy mouth the Lord Jesus, and shalt believe in thine heart that God hath raised him from the dead, thou shalt be saved" Rom. 10:9). It is stated in another place upon this wise—"He that believeth and is baptized shall be saved" (Mark 16:16)—that is Christ's way of making the confession of Him. If there be a true faith, there must be a declaration of it. If you are candles and God has lit you, "Let your light so shine before men, that they may see your good works, and glorify your Father which is in heaven" (Matt. 5:16). Soldiers of Christ must, like Her Majesty's soldiers, wear their regimentals. If they are ashamed of their regimentals, they ought to be drummed out of the regiment. They are not honest soldiers who refuse to march in rank with their comrades. The very least thing that the Lord Jesus Christ can expect of us is that we do confess Him to the best of our power. If you are nailed up to a cross, I will not invite you to be baptized. If you are fastened up to a tree to die, I will not ask you to come into this pulpit and declare your faith, for you cannot. But you are required to do what you can do, namely, to make as distinct and open avowal of the Lord Jesus Christ as may be suitable in your present condition.

I believe that many Christian people get into a deal of trouble through not being honest in their convictions. For instance, if a man goes into a workshop or a soldier into a barracks room, if he does not fly his flag from the first, it will be very difficult for him to run it up afterward. But if he immediately and boldly lets them know, "I am a Christian man, and there are certain things that I cannot do to please you and certain other things that I cannot help doing, though they displease you"—when that is clearly understood, after awhile the singularity of the thing will be gone and the man will be let alone. But if he is a little sneaky and thinks that he is going to please the world and please Christ too, he is in for a rough time, let him depend upon it. His life will be that of a toad under a harrow or a fox in a dog kennel if he tries the way of compromise. That will never do. Come out. Show your colors. Let it be known who you are and what you are. Although your course will not be smooth, it will certainly be not half so rough as if you tried to run with the hare and hunt with the hounds—a very difficult piece of business that.

This man came out, then and there, and made as open an avowal of his faith in Christ as was possible.

The next thing he did was to rebuke his fellow sinner. He spoke to him in answer to the ribaldry with which he had assailed our Lord. I do not know what the unconverted convict had been blasphemously saying, but his converted comrade spoke very honestly to him. "Dost not thou fear God, seeing thou art in the same condemnation? And we indeed justly; for we receive the due reward of or deeds: but this man hath done nothing amiss." It is more than ever needful in these days that believers in Christ should not allow sin to go unrebuked. Yet a great many of them do so. Do you not know that a person who is silent when a wrong thing is said or done may become a participator in the sin? If you do not rebuke sin—I mean, of course, on all fit occasions and in a proper spirit—your silence will give consent to the sin, and you will be an aider and abettor in it. A man who saw a robbery and who did not cry, "Stop thief!" would be thought to be in league with the thief. The man who can hear swearing or see impurity and never utter a word of protest may well question whether he is right himself. Other men's sins make up a great item in our personal guilt unless we in anywise rebuke them. This our Lord expects us to do. The dying thief did it and did it with all his heart. Therein he far exceeded large numbers of those who hold their heads high in the church.

Next, the dying thief made a full confession of his guilt. He said to him who was hanged with him, "Dost not thou fear God, seeing thou art in the same condemnation? And we indeed justly." Not many words, but what a world of meaning was in them—we indeed justly. "You and I are dying for our crimes," said he, "and we deserve to die." When a man is willing to confess that he deserves the wrath of God—that he deserves the suffering that his sin has brought upon him—there is evidence of sincerity in him. In this man's case, his repentance glittered like a holy tear in the eye of his faith so that his faith was bejeweled with the drops of his penitence. As I have often told you, I suspect the faith that is not born as a twin with repentance. But there is no room for suspicion in the case of this penitent confessor. I pray God that you and I may have such a thorough work as this in our own hearts as the result of our faith.

Then, this dying thief defends his Lord right manfully. He says, "We indeed justly; . . . but this man hath done nothing amiss." Was not that beautifully said? He did not say, "This man does not deserve to die," but "This man hath done nothing amiss." He means that He is perfectly innocent. He does not even say "He has done nothing wicked," but he even asserts that He has not acted unwisely or indiscreetly—This Man hath done nothing amiss. This is a glorious testimony of a dying man to one who was numbered with the transgressors and was being put to death because His enemies falsely accused Him. Beloved, I only pray that you and I may bear as good witness to our Lord as this thief did. He outruns us all. We need not think much of the coming of his conversion late in life. We may far rather consider how blessed was the testimony that he bore for his Lord when it was most needed. When all other voices were silent, one suffering penitent spoke out and said, "This man hath done nothing amiss."

See, again, another mark of this man's faith. *He prays and his prayer is directed to Jesus.* "Lord, remember me when thou comest into thy kingdom." True faith is always praying faith. "Behold, he prayeth," is one of the surest tests of the new birth. Oh, friends, may we abound in prayer, for thus we shall prove that our faith in Jesus Christ is what it ought to be! This converted robber opened his mouth wide in prayer. He prayed with great confidence as to the coming kingdom, and he sought that kingdom first, even to the exclusion of all else. He might have asked for life or for ease from pain, but he prefers the kingdom. This is a high mark of grace.

In addition to thus praying, you will see that *he adores and worships Jesus,* for he says, "Lord, remember me when thou comest into thy kingdom." The petition is worded as if he felt, "Only let Christ think of me, and it is enough. Let Him but remember me, and the thought of His mind will be effectual for everything that I shall need in the world to come." This is to impute Godhead to Christ. If a man can cast his all upon the mere memory of a person, he must have a very high esteem of that person. If to be remembered by the Lord Jesus is all that this man asks or desires, he pays to the Lord great honor. I think that there was about his prayer a worship equal to the eternal hallelujahs of cherubim and seraphim. There was in it a glorification of his Lord that is not excelled even by the endless symphonies of angelic spirits who surround the throne. Thief, you have done well!

Oh, that some penitent spirit here might be helped thus to believe, thus to confess, thus to defend his Master, thus to adore, thus to worship. Then the age of the convert would be a matter of the smallest imaginable consequence.

Our Lord's Word to This Man about the World to Come

Now, the last remark is this: There was something very special about the dying thief as to our Lord's word to him about the world to come. He said to him, "To day shalt thou be with me in paradise." He only asked the Lord to remember him, but he obtained this surprising answer, "To day shalt thou be with me in Paradise."

In some respects I envy this dying thief, the reason being that when the Lord pardoned me and pardoned the most of you who are present, He did not give us a place in paradise that same day. We are not yet come to the rest that is promised to us. No, you are waiting here. Some of you have been waiting very long. It is thirty years with many of us. It is forty years, it is fifty years with many others since the Lord blotted out your sins, and yet you are not with Him in paradise. There is a dear member of this church who, I suppose, has known the Lord for seventy-five years. She is still with us, having long passed the ninetieth year of her age. The Lord did not admit her to paradise on the day of her conversion. He did not take any one of us from nature to grace and from grace to glory in a day. We have had to wait a good while. There is something for us to do in the wilderness, and so we are kept out of the heavenly garden.

I remember that Mr. Baxter said that he was not in a hurry to be gone to heaven. A friend called upon Dr. John Owen, who had been writing about the glory of Christ, and asked him what he thought of going to heaven. That great divine replied, "I am longing to be there." "Why," said the other, "I have just spoken to holy Mr. Baxter, and he says that he would prefer to be here, since he thinks that he can be more useful on earth." "Oh!" said Dr. Owen, "my brother Baxter is always full of practical godliness, but for all that I cannot say that I am at all desirous to linger in this mortal state. I would rather be gone." Each of these men seems to me to have been the half of Paul. Paul was made up of the two, for he was desirous to depart, but he was willing to remain because it was needful for the people. We would put both together, and, like Paul, have a strong desire to depart and to be with Christ and yet be willing to wait if we can do service to our Lord and to His church.

Still, I think he has the best of it who is converted and enters heaven the same night. This robber breakfasted with the Devil, but he dined with Christ on earth and supped with Him in paradise. This was short work but blessed work. What a host of troubles he escaped! What a world of temptation he missed! What an evil world he quitted! He was just born, like a lamb dropped in the field, and then he was lifted into the Shepherd's bosom straight away. I do not remember the Lord ever saying this to anybody else. I dare say it may have happened that souls have been converted and have gone home at once. But I never heard of anybody that had such an assurance from Christ as this man had: "Verily, I say unto thee"; such a personal assurance: "Verily I say unto thee, To day shalt thou be with me in paradise." Dying thief, you were favored above many, to be with Christ, which is far better, and to be with Him so soon!

Why is it that our Lord does not thus emparadise all of us at once? It is because there is something for us to do on earth. My brethren, are you doing it? *Are you doing it?* Some good people are still on earth. But why? But why? What is the use of them? I cannot make it out. If they are indeed the Lord's people, what are they here for? They get up in the morning and eat their breakfast and in due course eat their dinner and their supper and go to bed and sleep. At a proper hour they get up the next morning and do the same as on the previous day. Is this living for Jesus? Is this life? It does not come to much. Can this be the life of God in man? Oh, Christian people, do justify your Lord in keeping you waiting here! How can you justify Him but by serving Him to the utmost of your power? The Lord help you to do so! Why, you owe as much to Him as the dying thief! I know I owe a great deal more. What a mercy it is to have been converted while you were yet a boy, to be brought to the Savior while you were yet a girl! What a debt of obligation young Christians owe to the Lord! And if this poor thief crammed a life full of testimony into a few minutes, ought not you and I, who are spared for years after conversion, to perform good service for our Lord? Come, let us wake up if we have been asleep! Let us begin to live if we have been half dead. May the Spirit of God make something of us yet so that we may go as industrious servants from the labors of the vineyard to the pleasures of the paradise! To our once crucified Lord be glory forever and ever! Amen.

5

The Centurion's Faith and Humility

Then Jesus went with them. And when he was now not far from the house, the centurion sent friends to him, saying unto him, Lord, trouble not thyself: for I am not worthy that thou shouldest enter under my roof: wherefore neither thought I myself worthy to come unto thee: but say in a word, and my servant shall be healed. For I also am a man set under authority, having under me soldiers, and I say unto one, Go, and he goeth; and to another, Come, and he cometh; and to my servant, Do this, and he doeth it (Luke 7:6–8).

The greatest light may enter into the darkest places. We may find the choicest flowers blooming where we least expected them. Here was a Gentile, a Roman, a soldier—a soldier clothed with absolute power—and yet a tender master, a considerate citizen, a lover of God! Let no man, therefore, be despised because of his calling, and let not the proverb, "Can there any good come out of Nazareth?" (John 1:46) be ever heard from the wise man's lips. The best of pearls have been found in the darkest caves of ocean. Why should it not be so still that God should have even in Sardis a few that have not defiled their garments, who shall walk with Christ in white, for they are worthy? Let no man think that because of his position in society he cannot excel in virtue. It is not the place that is to blame, but the man. If your heart be right, the situation may be difficult, but the difficulty is to be overcome. Aye, and out of that difficulty shall arise an excellence that you had not otherwise known. Say not in your heart, "I am a soldier, and the barracks room cannot minister to piety. Therefore I may live as I list because I cannot live as I should." Say not, "I am a working man in the

This sermon was taken from *The Metropolitan Tabernacle Pulpit* and was preached on Sunday morning, March 15, 1868.

midst of those who blaspheme, and therefore it were vain for me to talk of holiness and piety." No, rather remember that in such a case it is your duty specially not to talk of these precious things but to wear them about you as your daily ornament. Where should the lamp be placed but in the room that else were dark? Rest assured your calling and your position shall be no excuse for your sin if you continue therein. Neither shall your condition be any apology for the absence of integrity and virtue, if these be not found in you.

Concerning the centurion, we may remark that perhaps we had never heard of him, though he loved his servant. Perhaps we had never read his name, though he tenderly nursed his slave. Peradventure, he had found no place in the record of inspiration, though he loved the Jewish nation and built them a synagogue, nor had we read the story of his life, though he had become a proselyte to the Jewish faith. The one thing that gives him a place in these sacred pages is this, that he was a believer in the Messiah, that he was such a believer in the Son of God that Jesus said concerning him, "I have not found so great faith, no, not in Israel" (v. 9). There is the vital point. There, my hearer, is the notable matter that shall enroll you among the blessed. If you believe in Jesus Christ, the Son of God, your name is in the Lamb's book of life. But if you believe not in Him, your outward excellences, however admirable, shall avail you little.

The faith of the centurion is described, both in the eighth chapter of Matthew and in the chapter before us, as being of the highest kind, and the remarkable point in it is that it was coupled with the very deepest humility. The same man who said, "Say in a word, and my servant shall be healed," also said, "I am not worthy that thou shouldest enter under my roof." In bringing before you this noble soldier's example, these are two pivots upon which the discourse shall turn. I shall direct you to this double star, shining with so mild a radiance in the sky of Scripture: *This man's deep humility was not injurious to the strength of his faith,* and *his gigantic faith was by no means hostile to his deep humiliation.*

The Humility of the Centurion Was Not Injurious to the Strength of His Faith

Observe the centurion's humble expressions—he avowed that he was not worthy to come to Jesus. "Neither," said he, "thought I myself worthy to come unto thee." Then he further felt that he was not worthy that Jesus should come to him. "I am not worthy that thou shouldest enter under my roof." Was this self-abasement occasioned by the remembrance that he was a Gentile? That may have contributed to it. Was it because he was penitent on account of sundry rough and boisterous deeds that had stained his soldier life? It may be so. Was it not far rather because he had had a deep insight into his own heart and had learned to see sin in its true colors? Therefore he, who was worthy according to the statement of the Jews, was most unworthy in his own apprehension.

You may have noticed in the biography of some eminent men how badly they speak of themselves. Southey, in his *Life of Bunyan,* seems at a difficulty to understand how Bunyan could have used such depreciating language concerning his own character. For it is true, according to all we know of his biography, that he was not, except in the case of profane swearing, at all so bad as the most of the villagers. Indeed, there were some virtues in the man that were worthy of all commendation. Southey attributes it to a morbid state of mind, but we rather ascribe it to a return of spiritual health. Had the excellent poet seen himself in the same heavenly light as that in which Bunyan saw himself, he would have discovered that Bunyan did not exaggerate but was simply stating as far as he could a truth that utterly surpassed his powers of utterance. The great light that shone around Saul of Tarsus was the outward type of that inner light above the brightness of the sun which flashes into a regenerate soul and reveals the horrible character of the sin that dwells within. Believe me, when you hear Christians making abject confessions, it is not that they are worse than others, but that they see themselves in a clearer light than others. This centurion's unworthiness was not because he had been more vicious than other men—on the contrary, he had evidently been much more virtuous than the common run of mankind—but because he saw what others did not see and felt what others had not felt.

Deep as was this man's contrition, overwhelming as was his sense of utter worthlessness, he did not doubt for a moment either the power or the willingness of Christ. As for the question of willingness, it does not come under remark at all. The leper aforetime had said, "If thou wilt." But the centurion was so clear about Christ's willingness to relieve suffering humanity that it does not occur to him to mention it. He has long ago settled that matter and now takes it for granted as a very axiom in the knowledge of Jesus, for such a one as He must be willing to do all the good that is asked of Him.

Nor is he at all dubious about our Lord's power. The palsy that afflicted the servant was a remarkably grievous one, but it did not at all stagger the centurion. He felt not only that Jesus could heal it, could heal it at once, could heal it completely, but that He could heal it without moving a step from the place whereon He stood. Let but the word be uttered and in an instant his servant shall be healed. O glorious humiliation, how low you stoop! O noble faith, how high you soar! Brethren and sisters, if we can imitate this noble character in both respects—in the depth of his foundation, in the height of his pinnacle— how near to the model of the temple of God shall we be built up! Empty indeed he was, having nothing of his own—not worthy to receive, much less indulging a thought of giving anything to Christ. Yet he was confident that all things are possible with the Master and that He both can and will do according to our faith and that in a manner gloriously unveiling His kingly power.

My dear friends, especially you who are under concern of soul, you feel unworthy—that is not a mistaken feeling, you are so. You are much distressed by reason of this unworthiness, but if you knew more of it you might be more distressed still. The apprehension that you already have of your sinfulness, although it be very painful, does not at all reach to the full extent of it. You are much more sinful than you think you are, much more unworthy than you yet know yourself to be. Instead of attempting a foolish and wicked soothing of your dark thoughts and saying, "You have morbid ideas of yourself. You ought not so to speak," I rather pray you to believe that yours is an utterly hopeless case apart from Christ, that in your spiritual nature the whole head is sick and the whole heart faint. I want you not to film the horrible ulcer of your depravity with specious hopes and professions. I desire you not to look upon this disease as though it were but skin deep. It lies in the source and fountain of your life and poisons your heart. The flames of hell must wrap themselves about you assuredly unless Christ interpose to save you. You have no merit of any kind or sort, nor will you ever have any. And more, you have no power to escape from your lost condition unaided by the Savior's hand. Without Christ you can do nothing, for you are abjectly poor, bankrupt hopelessly, and you cannot by the utmost diligence make yourself any other than you are. No words that I can utter can exaggerate your deplorable condition, and no feelings that you can ever experience can represent your real state in colors too alarming. You are not worthy that Christ should come to you. You are not worthy to draw near to Christ. But, and here is a glorious contrast, never let this for a single moment interfere with your full belief that He who is God but who took our nature, that He who suffered in our stead upon the cross, that He who now rules in the highest heavens is able to do for you and willing to do for you exceeding abundantly above what you ask or even think. Your inability does not prevent the working of His power. Your unworthiness cannot put fetters to His bounty or limits to His grace. You may be an ill-deserving sinner, but that is no reason why He should not pardon you. You may be in your own apprehension, and truthfully so, the most unworthy that He ever stooped to bless, yet this is no reason why He should not condescend to press you to His bosom, to accept and to save you. I wish that as the first truth has impressed itself deeply upon you, the second truth may with equal force take up the possession of your heart, and that is that Jesus Christ is able to save to the uttermost them that come unto God by Him and is as willing as He is able (see Heb. 7:25). Your emptiness does not affect His fullness. Your weakness does not alter His power. Your inability does not diminish His omnipotence. Your undesert does not restrain the bowels of His love that freely move toward the very vilest of the vile.

By some means Satan almost always manages it this way, that when we get a little hope it is generally a self-grounded hope, a vain idea that we are getting better in ourselves—a mischievous conceit: proud flesh, which hinders the cure and which the Surgeon must cut out. It has no sign of healing; it prevents healing. On the other hand, if we obtain a deep sense of sin, the Evil One manages to put his hoof in there and to insinuate that Jesus is not able to save such as we are—a great falsehood, for who shall say what the limit of Christ's power is? But if these two things could but meet together, a thorough sense of sin and an immovable belief in the power of Christ to grapple with sin and to overcome it, surely the kingdom of heaven would then have come near to us in power and in truth. It would be again said, "I have not found so great faith, no, not in Israel" (Luke 7:9).

Now, you troubled hearts, I have this word for you, and then I shall pass on to another point. Your sense of your unworthiness, if it be properly used, should drive you to Christ. You are unworthy, but Jesus died for the unworthy. Jesus did not die for those who profess to be by nature good and deserving, for the whole have no need of a physician. But it is written, "In due time Christ died for the ungodly" (Rom. 5:6). "[He] gave himself for our"—what? Excellences and virtues? No; "[He] gave himself for our sins" (Gal. 1:4), according to the Scriptures. We read that He "suffered the just for the"—for the just? By no means, "the just for the unjust" (1 Peter 3:18), to bring us to God. Gospel pharmacy is for the sick; Gospel bread is for the hungry; Gospel fountains are open to the unclean; Gospel water is given to the thirsty. You who need not shall not have, but you who want it may freely come. Let your huge and painful wants impel you to fly to Jesus. Let the vast cravings of your insatiable spirit compel you to come to Him in whom all fullness dwells. Your unworthiness should act as a wing to bear you to Christ, the sinner's Savior.

It should also have this effect upon you: it should prevent your raising those scruples and making those demands that are such a hindrance to some persons finding peace. The proud spirit says, "I must have signs and wonders, or I will not believe. I must feel deep convictions and horrible tremors, or I must quake because of dreams or threatening texts applied to me with awful power." Ah! but, unworthy one, if you be truly humbled, you will not dare to ask for these. You will have done with demands and stipulations and will cry, "Lord, give me but a word, speak but a word of promise, and it shall be enough for me. Do but say to me, 'Thy sins are forgiven thee.' Give me but half a text, give me one kind, assuring word to sink my fears again, and I will believe it and rest upon it." Thus your sense of unworthiness should lead you to a simple faith in Jesus and prevent your demanding those manifestations that the foolish so eagerly and impudently require. Beloved, it has come to this: you are so unworthy that you are shut out of every hope but Christ. All other doors are fast nailed against you. If there be anything to be done for salvation, you cannot do it. If there be any fitness wanted, you have it not. Christ comes to you and tells you that there is no fitness wanted for coming to Him but that if you will but trust Him He will save you. I think I hear you say, Then, my Lord, since it has come to this,

> I can but perish if I go;
> I am resolved to try;
> For if I stay away, I know
> I must forever die.

And so, sink or swim, upon Your precious atonement I cast my guilty soul, persuaded that You are able to save even such a one as I am. I am so thoroughly persuaded of the goodness of Your heart that I know You will not cast away a poor trembler who comes to You and takes You to be his only ground of trust.

The Centurion's Great Faith
Was Not Hostile to His Humility

The centurion's faith was extraordinary. It ought not to be extraordinary. we ought all of us to believe as well in Christ as this soldier did. Observe the form it took. He said to himself, "I am a subaltern officer under authority. I am not the commander in chief, I am merely the commander of a troop of a hundred men. Yet over those hundred men I exert unlimited control. I say to this one, Go, and he goes. I say to the other 'Come,' and he comes. My servant, my poor sick servant [his tender heart comes back to him, and he puts him into the illustration], I say to him, 'Do this,' and he does it at once. I am simply a petty officer under authority myself. But such is the influence of discipline that there are no questions raised, no deliberations tolerated. No soldier turns around and tells me that I have set him too difficult a task. No one out of all the troop ever dares to say to me 'I shall not do it.'" The power of discipline among the legions of Rome was exceedingly great. The commander had but to say, "Do it," and it was done, though thousands bled and died. "Now," argued the centurion, "This glorious man is the Son of God. He is not a subaltern. He is the commander in chief. If He gives the word, His will most surely must be done. Fevers and paralysis, good influences and bad, they must be all under His control. He can therefore heal my servant in a moment."

Who can resist the great Caesar of heaven and earth? That was, I believe, the centurion's idea. Jesus has therefore but to will it, and to the utmost bounds of the earth those influences that are under His control will at once set to work to perform His will. The centurion pictured himself as sitting down in the house and effecting his desires without rising by merely issuing an order. His faith placed the Lord Jesus in the same position. "You need not come to my dwelling; You can stand here, and if You will but say it, the cure will be wrought at once." He did in his heart enthrone the Lord Jesus as a captain over all the forces of the world, as the generalissimo of heaven and earth—as, in fact, the Caesar, the imperial governor of all the forces of the universe. 'Twas graciously thought, 'twas poetically embodied, 'twas nobly spoken, 'twas gloriously believed, but it was the truth and nothing more than the truth, for universal dominion is really in the power of Jesus today. If He were a true Caesar before He died, while He was despised and rejected of men, much more now that He has trodden through the winepress and stained His vesture with the blood of His vanquished enemies, much more now that He has led captivity captive and sits enthroned by filial right at the right hand of God, even the Father, much more now that God has sworn that He will put all things under His feet and that at the name of Jesus every knee shall bow of things in heaven and things on earth and things that are under the earth. Much more, I say, can He now work according to His good pleasure. He has today but to speak and it is done, to command and it shall stand fast.

Beloved, see whether this truth bears us as on eagle's wings. Caesar has but to say, *Absolvo te,* and his guilty subject is acquitted. Caesar has but to speak and a province is conquered, an army routed. Stormy seas are navigated at Caesar's bidding, mountains are tunneled, the whole world shall be girded with military roads. Caesar is absolute, and his will is law. So on earth, but so much more in heaven. Let the imperial Caesar of heaven but say, "I forgive," and the devils of hell cannot accuse you. Let Him say, "I will help you," and who shall oppose? If Emmanuel be for you, who shall be against you? Let Him speak and the bonds of sinful habit must fall off, and the darkness in which your soul has long been immured must give place to instantaneous light. He reigns as King, Lord over all. Let His name be blessed forever. Let each one of us, by our faith, give Him the honor that is due to His name. All hail! great Emperor, once slain but now forever Lord of heaven and earth!

Here is one point to which I recall you. This man's faith did not for a moment interfere with his thorough personal humiliation—interfere with it! My friends, it was the source of it; it was the very foundation on which it rested. Do you not see, the higher his thoughts of Christ, the more unworthy he felt himself to be of the kind attentions of so good and great a personage? If he had thought less of Jesus, he would not have said, "I am not worthy that thou shouldest enter under my roof." There was, of course, a sight of himself to humble him, but the far more wondrous vision of the glory of the Lord Jesus was the true root and parent of his self-abasement. Because Christ was so great, he felt himself to be unworthy either to meet Him or entertain Him.

Observe, my brethren and sisters, his faith acted upon his humility by making him content with a word from Christ. His faith said, "A word is enough. It will work the cure." Then his humility said, "Ah, how unworthy I am even of so little a thing as a word. If a word will work a miracle, it is so great and powerful a thing that it is more than I deserve. Therefore," said he, "I will not ask for more. I will not ask for footsteps when a sound will suffice. I will not clamor for His presence when His wish can restore my servant to health. "His believing that a word was enough made him humbly decline to pray for more so that his confidence in Christ, instead of interfering with his sense of unworthiness, aided its manifestation. Brethren and sisters, never think for a moment, as many foolish persons do, that strong faith in the Lord is necessarily pride—it is the reverse. It is one of the worst forms of pride to question the promise of God. When a man says, "Christ has promised to save those who trust Him. I have trusted Him, therefore I am saved. I know I am. I am sure of it because God says so, and I do not want any better evidence." That assurance is humility in action. But if a man says, "God has said that those who trust Him shall be saved. I do trust Him, but still I do not know that I am saved." Why, you do as much as say you do not know whether God is a liar or not. What can be more impertinent, what can be more proudly insulting than that?

I know it is a most common thing to say, "It seems so presumptuous to say I know I am saved." I think it far more presumptuous to doubt when God speaks positively and to mistrust where the promise is plain. God says, "He that believeth and is baptized shall be saved" (Mark 16:16). If you believe and are baptized, if God be true, you shall be saved—you are saved. There is no hoping about it—it must be so. Let God be true and every man a liar. Far off from these lips be the insinuation of a doubt that perhaps God can be false to His promise and may break His word. If you question anything, question whether you do trust Christ, but that settled, the question is ended. It you believe that Jesus is the Christ, you are born of God. If you rest alone on Him, your sins, which are many, are all forgiven. Take God at His word as your child takes you at your word. It is not too much for God to ask; you ask it of your child. Though you be a poor fallible creature, you would not have your child mistrust you. Shall you be believed and not your God? Shall your little one be expected to confide in you though you are evil, and will you not believe the voice of your heavenly parent to be the very truth and rest upon it? Ah! do so, I beseech you, and the more you do it, the more you will feel your unworthiness to do so. For it astounds me to think that I shall be saved. It amazes me to think I shall be washed from my every sin in the precious blood of Christ, that I shall be set upon a rock, and a new song shall be put into my mouth. It astounds me, and as I think of it, I say, "How unworthy I am of such favors! I am less than the least of all the benefits that you have bestowed upon me." Your faith will not murder your humility, your humility will not stab at your faith. But the two will go hand in hand to heaven like a brave brother and a fair sister—the one bold as a lion the other meek as a dove, the one rejoicing in Jesus the other blushing at self. Blessed pair, fain would I entertain you in my heart all the days of my pilgrimage on earth.

I have thus, as best I could, brought before you the example of the centurion with a few incidental lessons. Now to apply it with as much earnestness and brevity as we can summon. The application shall be to three sorts of people.

The Application to Distressed Minds

First, we speak to distressed minds deeply conscious of their unworthiness. Jesus Christ is able and willing to save you this very morning. What is the form of your distress? Is it that your sins are great? Believe, I charge you, and may God the Holy Spirit help you believe that all your sins Christ can pardon now. See Him upon yonder cross? He is divine, but how He bleeds! He is divine, but how He groans! He smarts! He dies! Do you believe that any sin is too great for those sufferings to put away? Do you think the Son of God offered an inadequate atonement?—an atonement of which you can say there is a limit to its efficacy beyond which it cannot operate for the salvation of believers, so that after all, sin is greater than the sacrifice, and the filth is more full of defilement than the blood is of purification? O crucify not Christ afresh by doubting the power of the eternal God!

My friends, when in the stillness of the starry night we look up to the orbs of heaven and remember the marvelous truths that astronomy has revealed to us of the magnificence, the inconceivable majesty of creation, if we then reflect that the infinite God who made all these became man for us and that as man He was fastened to the transverse wood and that He bled to death for us, why it will appear to us that if all the stars were crowded with inhabitants and all those inhabitants had all been rebellious against God and had steeped themselves up to the very throat in scarlet crimes, there must be efficacy enough in the blood of such a one as God Himself incarnate to take all their sins away. For this great miracle of miracles, God Himself paying honor to His own justice by suffer-

ing a substitutionary death, is an exhibition of infinite severity and love
that, far down eternity, must appear so glorious as utterly to swallow up
the remembrance of creature sin and to put it altogether out of sight. Yes,
sinner, believe you that this moment the sins of fifty years can drop from
off you, aye, of seventy or eighty years—that in an instant, you who are
as black as hell can be pure as heaven if Jesus says the word. If you believe in Him it is done, for to trust Him is to be clean.

Perhaps, however, your difficulty is to get rid of a hardness of heart.
You feel that you cannot repent, but cannot Jesus make you repent by
His Spirit? Do you hesitate about that question? See the world a few
months ago hard bound with frost, but how daffodil and crocus and
snowdrop have come up above that once-frozen soil. How snow and ice
have gone, and the genial sun shines out! God does it readily with the
soft breath of the south wind and the kind sunbeam, and He can do the
same in the spiritual world for you. Believe He can and ask Him now to
do it, and you shall find that the rock of ice shall thaw. That huge, horrible, devilish iceberg of a heart of yours shall begin to drip with showers
of crystal penitence that God shall accept through His dear Son.

But, perhaps, it is some bad habit that gives you trouble. You have been
long in it. Can the Ethiopian change his skin or the leopard his spots? You
cannot get rid of it. I know you cannot. It is a desperate evil. It drags you
downward like the hands of demons pulling you from the surface of life's
stream down into its black and horrid depths of death and defilement. Ah!
I know your dreads and despairs. But man, I ask you, cannot Jesus deliver? He has the key of your heart, and He can turn it so that all its wheels
shall revolve otherwise than now. He who shakes the earth with earth-
quake and sweeps the sea with tornado can send a heartquake and a storm
of strong repentance and tear up your old habits by the roots. He whose
every act is wonderful can surely do what He will within this the little
world of your soul, since in the great world outside He rules as He pleases.
Believe in His power and ask Him to prove it. He has but to say in a word,
and this matter of present distress shall be taken away. Still I hear you say,
"I cannot"; a horrible inability hangs over you. But it is not what you can
do or cannot do—these have nothing to do with it—it is what Jesus can
do. Can there be anything too hard for the Lord? Can the eternal Spirit
ever be defeated when He wills to conquer in a man? Can He who "bears
the earth's huge pillars up, and spreads the heavens abroad," who once
was crucified but who now ever lives, can He fail? Put your care into His
hand, poor, unable wretch, and ask Him to do for you what you cannot do
for yourself and according to your faith so shall it be to you.

The Application to Patient Workers

A second application of our subject shall be made to the patient workers who are ready to faint. I know that in this house there are many who incessantly plead with God for their unconverted relatives and neighbors that they may be saved. You have pleaded long for your husband and your son and your daughter, but they have gone yet further into sin. Instead of answers to prayer, it seems as though heaven laughed at your importunity. Take heed of one thing: do not suffer unbelief to make you think that the object of your care cannot be saved. While there is life there is hope. Yes, though they add drunkenness to lust and blasphemy to drunkenness and hardness of heart and impenitence to blasphemy, Jesus has but to say the word and they shall be turned, every one, from their evil way. Under the use of the means of grace it may be done, or even without the means it may be done. There have been men at work or at their amusements, all in their wickedness, who have had impressions that have made them new men when it was least expected such a thing would occur. Those who have been the ringleaders in Satan's rebellious crew have frequently become the boldest captains in the army of Christ. There is no room for doubt as to the possibility of the salvation of anybody when Jesus gives the word of command. You are unchristian when you shut out the harlot from hope, when you exclude the thief from repentance, when you even despair of the murderer. The big heart of God is greater than all your hearts put together, and the great thoughts of the loving Father are not as your thoughts when they climb the highest. Neither are His ways your ways when they are at their utmost liberality. Oh, if your friend, your child, your wife, your husband be a very devil incarnate or if there be seven devils, or a legion of devils within your loved one, while Christ lives never mutter the word *despair*. He can cast out the legion of evil spirits and impart His Holy Spirit instead thereof. Therefore have faith. You are unworthy to receive the blessing, but have faith in Him who is so able to bestow it.

Many of you are going to your classes this afternoon, others of you will be engaged this evening in preaching the Gospel, and you are getting very fainthearted because you do not see the success you so much desire. Well, perhaps it is good for you to feel how little you can do apart from the divine ministrations. May this humiliation of soul continue, but do not let it degenerate into a distrust of Him. If Christ were dead and buried and had never risen, it were a horrible case for us poor preachers. But while Christ lives, endowed with the residue of the eternal Spirit that He freely gives we ought not so much as fear, much less despair. May the church of God pluck up heart and feel that with a living Christ in the midst of her armies victory shall before long wait upon her banners.

The Application to Weary Watchers

The last application I shall make is the same as the second, only on a wider scale. There are many who are like watchers who have grown weary. We have heard that Christ is coming—the great coming man. The Lord knows right well that there is pressing need for someone to come, for this poor old machine of a world creaks dreadfully and seems as though it were so laden with the sheaves of human sin that its axles would snap. God's infinite long-suffering has kept a crazy world from utter dissolution by a thousand helps and stays, but it is poor work and seems to get worse and worse. Our state is rotten at the very core both in business and politics. No man seems to succeed so well as he who has dispensed with his conscience and laughs at principles. All things are come to that point that there is need for some deliverer to come, or else I do not know where we shall all go to. But He will come, so the promise stands. To those who wait for Him, His coming shall be as the beams of the daystar proclaiming the dawn. He is coming. At His coming there shall be a glorious time, a millennium, a period of light and truth and joy and holiness and peace. We are watching and waiting for it.

But we say, "Ah, it is hopeless to think of converting the world! How is the truth to be preached? Where are the tongues to speak it? How few proclaim it boldly? Where are the men to carry Christ's Cross to the utmost bounds of the globe and conquer nations for Him?" Ah, say not in your heart, the former days were better than now. Write not a book of lamentation and say, "The prophets, where are they? The apostles have gone and all the mighty confessors who lived and died for Christ have disappeared." At the lifting of His finger the Lord can raise up a thousand Jonahs for every city throughout the land, a thousand bold Isaiahs to declare His glory. He has but to bid it and companies of apostles and armies of martyrs shall start up from the quiet nooks of old England villages or shall pour forth from the workshops of her cities. He can do wonders when He wills it. The worst plight of the church is but the time when her flood has ebbed in order that it may return in the fullness of its strength. Have confidence, for even should the instruments fail and the ministry become a dead and effete thing, yet His coming shall accomplish His purposes. When He appears, the kingdoms of this world shall become the kingdoms of our Lord and of His Christ.

Jesus is not under authority, but He has soldiers under Him, and He has but to say to this spirit or to that, "Go," or "Come," and His will shall be done. He has but to quicken His church by His Holy Spirit and say, "Do this," and the impossible task shall be accomplished. What seemed beyond all human skill or mortal hope shall be wrought and wrought at once. When He says, "Do," it shall be done and His name shall be praised. O for more faith and more self-abasement. Twin angels, abide in this assembly evermore. Go forth with us to battle and return with us from the victory. O Lord, the lover of humility and the author of faith, give us to be steeped in both for Jesus' sake. Amen.

6

Joseph of Arimathea

Joseph of Arimathaea, an honourable counsellor, which also waited for the kingdom of God, came, and went in boldly unto Pilate, and craved the body of Jesus. And Pilate marvelled if he were already dead: and calling unto him the centurion, he asked him whether he had been any while dead. And when he knew it of the centurion, he gave the body to Joseph. And he bought fine linen, and took him down, and wrapped him in the linen, and laid him in a sepulchre which was hewn out of a rock, and rolled a stone unto the door of the sepulchre (Mark 15:43–46).

It was a very dark day with the church of God and with the cause of Christ, for the Lord Jesus was dead, and so the sun of their souls had set. "All the disciples forsook him, and fled" (Matt. 26:56). "Ye shall be scattered, every man to his own, and shall leave me alone" (John 16:32), were the sad words of Jesus, and they had come true. He was dead upon the cross, and His enemies hoped that there was an end of Him, while His friends feared that it was even so. A few women who had remained about the cross, true to the very last, were found faithful to death. But what could they do to obtain His sacred body and give it honorable burial? That priceless flesh seemed to be in danger of the fate that usually awaited the bodies of malefactors. At any rate, the fear was that it might be hurled into the first grave that could be found to shelter it.

At that perilous moment Joseph of Arimathea, a city of the Jews, of whom we never heard before and of whom we never hear again, suddenly made his appearance. He was the very man needed for the occasion, a man of influence. He was a man possessing that kind of influence that was most potent with Pilate—a rich man, a counselor, a

---

This sermon was taken from *The Metropolitan Tabernacle Pulpit* and was preached on Sunday morning, July 6, 1884.

member of the Sanhedrim, a person of weight and character. Every evangelist mentions him and tells us something about him. From these we learn that he was a disciple, "a good man and a just; . . . who also himself waited for the kingdom of God." Joseph had been retiring and, probably, cowardly before. But now he came to the cross and saw how matters stood and then went in boldly to Pilate, craved the body of Jesus, and obtained it.

Let us learn from this that God will always have His witnesses. It matters not though the ministry should forsake the truth, though they that should be leaders should become recreant, the truth of God will not fail for lack of friends. It may be with the church as when a standard-bearer faints and the host is ready to melt with dismay, but there shall be found other standard-bearers and the banner of the Lord shall wave over all. As the Lord lives, so shall His truth live. As God reigns, so shall the Gospel reign, even though it be from the cross. "Tell it out among the heathen that the Lord reigneth from the tree." Such is a singular version of a verse in the Psalms, and it contains a glorious truth. Even while Jesus hangs on the cross in death, He is still keeping possession of the throne, and He shall reign forever and ever.

Let this be remembered for your encouragement in the cloudy and dark day. If you live in any place where the faithful fail from among men, do not wring your hands in grief and sit down in despair as though it was all over with the cause you love. The Lord lives and will yet keep a faithful seed alive in the earth. Another Joseph of Arimathea will come forward at the desperate moment. Just when we cannot do without him the man will be found. There was a Joseph for Israel in Egypt, and there was a Joseph for Jesus on the cross. A Joseph acted to Him a father's part at His birth, and another Joseph arranged for His burial. The Lord shall not be left without friends. There was a dark day in the Old Testament history when the eyes of Eli, the servant of God, had failed him. Worse still, he was almost as blind mentally as physically, for his sons made themselves vile, and he restrained them not. It seemed as if God must forsake His Israel. But who is this little boy who is brought in by his mother? this tiny child who is to be left in the sanctuary to serve his God as long as he lives? this pretty little man who wears the little coat that his mother's hands have lovingly made for him? Look, you that have eyes of faith, for the prophet Samuel is before you, the servant of the Lord, by whose holy example Israel shall be led to better things and delivered from the oppression that chastised the iniquities of Eli's sons.

God has today somewhere, I know not where, in yon obscure cottage of an English village or in a log hut far away in the backwoods of America or in the slums of our back streets or in our palaces, a man who in maturer life shall deliver Israel, fighting the battles of the Lord. The Lord has His servant making ready, and when the time shall come, when the hour shall want the man, the man shall be found for the hour. The Lord's will shall be done, let infidels and doubters think what they please. I see in this advent of Joseph of Arimathea exactly at the needed time a well of consolation for all who have the cause of God laid upon their hearts. We need not worry our heads about who is to succeed the pastors and evangelists of today. The apostolical succession we may safely leave with our God.

Concerning this Joseph of Arimathea, the honorable counselor, I want to speak this morning, praying that I may speak to your souls all along. As I have already said, we hear no more of Joseph than what is recorded here. He shines out when he is wanted, and anon he disappears. His record is on high. We need not mention the traditions about him, for I think that even the quotation of legends has an evil tendency and may turn us aside from the pure, unadulterated Word of God. What have you and I to do with tradition? Is not the Scripture enough? There is probably no truth in the silly tales about Joseph and Glastonbury. If there were, it would be of no consequence to us. If any fact had been worthy of the pen of inspiration, it would have been written. Because it is not written, we need not desire to know. Let us be satisfied to pause where the Holy Spirit stays His pen.

I shall use Joseph of Arimathea this morning in four ways: first, as *our warning*—he was a disciple of Jesus, "but secretly for fear of the Jews" (John 19:38); secondly, for *our instruction*—he was at last brought out by the cross, concerning which holy Simeon had declared that by the death of the Lord Jesus the thoughts of many hearts should be revealed; thirdly, for *our arousing*—there was an occasion for Joseph to come forward, and there is occasion now for all the timid to grow brave; and lastly, for *our guidance*—that we may, if we have been at all bashful and fearful, come forward in the hour of need and behave ourselves as bravely as Joseph of Arimathea did on the eve before the Paschal Sabbath.

Our Warning

He was a disciple of Christ, but secretly, for fear of the Jews. We do not advise any one of you to imitate Joseph in that. Fear that leads us to conceal our faith is an evil thing. Be a disciple by all means but not secretly. You miss a great part of your life's purpose if you are. Above all, do not be a disciple secretly because of the fear of man, for the fear of man brings a snare. If you are the slave of such fear it demeans you, belittles you, and prevents your giving due glory to God.

> Fear him, ye saints, and you will then
> Have nothing else to fear.

Be careful to give honor to Christ and He will take care of your honor.

Why was it that Joseph of Arimathea was so backward? Perhaps it was owing to *his natural disposition*. Many men are by nature very bold. Some are a little too much so, for they become intrusive, self-assertive, not to say impudent. I have heard of a certain class of persons who rush in where angels fear to tread. They are fearless because they are brainless. Let us avoid fault in that direction. Many, on the other hand, are too retiring. They have to screw their courage up even to say a good word for the Savior whom they love. If they can do so, they fall into the rear rank. They hope to be found among the victors when they divide the spoil, but they are not overambitious to be among the warriors while they are braving the foe. Some of these are truehearted notwithstanding their timidity. It was found in the martyr days that certain of those who endured most bravely at the stake were naturally of a fearful mind. It is noted by Foxe that some who boasted of how well they could bear pain and death for Christ turned tail and recanted, while others who in prison trembled at the thought of the fire played the man in death to the admiration of all that were around them. Still, dear friends, it is not a desirable thing if you are troubled with timidity to foster it at all. Fear of man is a plant to be rooted and not to be nurtured. I should set that plant, if I could, where it would get but little water and no sunshine, and meanwhile I would beg a cutting from a better tree. Would it not be well often to brace ourselves with such a hymn as this:

> Am I a soldier of the cross?
>   A follower of the Lamb?
> And shall I fear to own His cause,
>   Or blush to speak His name?
>
> Must I be carried to the skies
>   On flowery beds of ease,
> While others fought to win the prize
>   And sailed through bloody seas?

If you know that your temptation lies in the direction of fear, watch and strive against it. School yourselves evermore to dauntless courage by the help of the Holy Spirit.

I am afraid, too, that what helped to intimidate Joseph of Arimathea was the fact that he was *a rich man*. A sad truth lies within our Lord's solemn exclamation, "How hardly shall they that have riches enter into the kingdom of God!" (Luke 18:24). Riches do not strengthen the heart or make men daring for the good cause. Albeit wealth is a great talent that may be well used by the man who has entered into the kingdom of heaven, yet it brings with it snares and temptations. When a man has not yet entered into the kingdom it is, in many ways, a terrible hindrance to his entrance. "It is easier for a camel to go through the eye of a needle, than for a rich man to enter into the kingdom" (Matt. 19:24). The fishermen of the Galilean lake readily left their bits of boats and their fishing tackle, but Joseph of Arimathea was a rich man and was, therefore, slow to leave all for Christ's sake. The tendency of great possessions is seen in the case of the young man who turned away in sorrow from the Lord Jesus when put to the unusual test of selling all he had. Strong swimmers have saved their lives when the ship has struck upon a rock by casting aside every weight, while others have gone straight down to the bottom because they have bound their gold around their waists. Gold sinks men as surely as lead. Take care, any of you that are well to do in this world, that you do not permit the liberality of God to be a cause of disloyalty to Him. Beware of the pride of life, the lust for rank, the desire to hoard, for any of these may prevent your service of your Lord. Riches puff men up and prevent their stooping to find the pearl of great price. A poor man enters a humble village sanctuary where Christ is preached and finds eternal life. Another man under concern of soul in the same village does not like to go down to the poor conventicle and remains unblessed. He keeps away because he puts to himself the question, "What will the people say if the squire goes to hear the Gospel? What a stir there will be if the son of a lord is converted!" Joseph of Arimathea's wealth made him unduly cautious and possibly, without his knowing it, prevented his casting in his lot with the common sort of people who followed the Lord Jesus. His heart was for the prize, but the heavy weight of his substance hindered him in his race. It was an instance of abounding grace that he was helped to run well at the last.

Possibly, too, he may have been checked by the fact that *he was in office and that he was honorable in it.* It needs great grace to carry human honor. Truth to tell, it is not particularly much worth carrying when you have it. For what is fame but the breath of men's nostrils? poor stuff to feed a soul upon! If a man could so live as to gain universal plaudits, if he could write his name athwart the sky in letters of gold, what of it all? What is there in the applause of a thoughtless multitude? The approbation of good men, if it be gained by persevering virtue, is better to be desired than great riches. But even then it may become a temptation, for the man may begin to question rather, What will people say? than, What will God say? The moment he falls into that mood he has introduced a weakening element into his life. The

"Well done, good and faithful servant" (Matt. 25:23), of the Master's own lips is worth ten thousand thunders of applause from senators and princes. Honor among men is, at best, a peril to the best. Joseph was honored in council, and this is apt to make a man prudently slow. The tendency of office is toward caution rather than enthusiasm. I would have those placed in high positions remember this and candidly judge themselves as to whether their shrinking from the public avowal of Christ may not be a cowardice unworthy of the position in which the Lord has placed them.

It seems clear that all the earthly things that men covet may not be so desirable as they appear to be, and that which men would give their eyes to procure, they might, if their eyes were opened, think far less of.

I would lovingly inquire of you at this time (for the sermon is meant to be personal all the way through) if any of you who love my Lord and Master are doing so secretly because of the fear of men. You have never openly confessed your faith, and why not? What hinders your taking up a decided position on the Lord's side? Are you wealthy? Are you honorable? Do you occupy an enviable position in society? And are you such a mean-spirited creature that you have become proud of these glittering surroundings, like a child that is vain of its new frock? Are you so craven that you will not cast in your lot with the followers of truth and righteousness because they are persons of low degree? Are you really so base? Is there no holy chivalry in you? Can it be so, that, because God has dealt so well with you and trusted you so generously, you will repay Him by denying His Son, violating your conscience, and turning your back on truth, and all for the sake of being in the fashion? I know it may seem hard to receive the cold shoulder in society or to have the finger of scorn pointed at you. But to bow before this selfish dread is scarcely worthy of a man and utterly disgraceful to a Christian man. "Oh, but I am so retiring in disposition." Yes, but do not indulge it, I pray you. For, if all were of such a mind, where were the noble advances of truth, her reformations, her revivals? Where would have been our Luther or our Calvin or our Zwingle? Where would have been our Whitefield or our Wesley if they had thought it to be the main object of desire to walk at ease along the cool sequestered vale of life? Come forth, my brother and sister, for the truth and for the Lord. Recollect that what is right for you would be right for the rest of us. If you do not join the Christian church, for instance, every one of us might also neglect that duty, and where would be the visible church of Christ? How would the ordinances of our holy faith be kept up as a witness among the sons of men? I charge all concealed believers to think over the inconsistency of their concealment and to quit that cowardly condition.

I feel sure that Joseph of Arimathea was a great loser by his secrecy. You see, he did not live with Jesus, as many other disciples did. During that brief but golden period in which men walked and talked and ate and drank with Jesus, Joseph was not with Him. He was not among the Twelve as possibly he might have been if he had possessed more courage and decision. He lost many of those familiar talks with which the Lord indulged His own after the multitudes had been sent away. He missed that sacred training and strengthening which fitted men for the noble lives of primitive saints. How many opportunities he must have missed, too, of working for the Master and with the Master! Perhaps we hear no more of him because he had done no more. Possibly that one grand action that has redeemed his name from forgetfulness is all that is recorded because it really was all that was worth recording. Joseph must have been a weaker, a sadder, a less useful man for having followed Christ afar off. I would to God that such reflections as these would fetch out our beloved, truly faithful, and honorable Christian men who hitherto have hidden away among the stuff and have not come to the front to stand up for Jesus.

Our Instruction

Joseph did come out after all, and so will you, my friends. If you are honest and sincere, you will have to avow your Lord sooner or later. Do you not think it would be better to make it sooner rather than later? The day will come when that shame which you are now dreading will be yours. As surely as you are a sincere believer, you will have to encounter that reproach and derision that now alarm you. Why not face them at once and get it over? You will have to confess Christ before many witnesses; why not begin to do so at once? What is the hardship of it? It will come easier to you, will bring you a larger blessing, and will be sweeter in the recollection afterward than if you keep on postponing it. What was it that fetched Joseph of Arimathea out? *It was the power of the Cross!* Is it not a remarkable thing that all the life of Christ did not draw out an open avowal from this man? Our Lord's miracles, His marvelous discourses, His poverty and self-renunciation, His glorious life of holiness and benevolence all may have helped to build up Joseph in his secret faith, but it did not suffice to develop in him a bold avowal of faith. The shameful death of the Cross had greater power over Joseph than all the beauty of Christ's life.

Now let us see, you timid, backward ones, whether the Cross will not have the same influence over you today. I believe it will if you carefully study it. I am sure it will if the Holy Spirit lays it home to your heart. I suppose that to Joseph of Arimathea Christ's death on the cross seemed such *a wicked thing* that he must come out on behalf of one so evil entreated. He had not consented to the deed of the men of the Sanhedrim when they condemned Jesus to death. Probably he and Nicodemus withdrew themselves from the assembly altogether. But when he saw that the crime was actually committed and that the innocent man had been put to death, then he said, "I cannot be a silent witness of such a murder. I must now side with the holy and the just." Therefore he came out and was found the willing servant of his crucified Master. Come what may of it, he felt that he must own himself to be on the right side now that they had maliciously taken away the life of the Lord Jesus. It was late, it was sadly late, but it was not too late.

Oh, secret disciple, will you not quit your hiding place? Will you not hasten to do so? You who are quiet and retiring, when you hear the name of Jesus blasphemed, as it is in these evil days, will you not stand up for Him? When you hear His deity denied, when His headship in the church is given to another, when His very person is by lewd fellows of the baser sort set up as the target of their criticism, will you not speak up for Him? Will you not be shocked by such evil conduct into an open avowal? His cause is that of truth and righteousness and mercy and hope for the sons of men, therefore He must not be abused while you sit by in silence. Had others favored Him you might, perhaps, have been somewhat excused for holding back. But you cannot keep back without grievous sin now that so many deride Him. Jesus is worthy of all honor, and yet they heap scorn upon Him. Will you not defend Him? He is your Savior and Lord; oh, be not slow to own that you are His. The Cross laid bare the heart of Joseph. He loathed the wickedness that slew the Holy and the Just, and therefore he girded himself to become the guardian of His sacred body.

But, next, it may have been in part *the wonderful patience of the Master's death* that made Joseph feel he could not hide any longer. Did he hear Him say, "Father, forgive them; for they know not what they do" (Luke 23:34)? Did he mark Him when those blessed lips said, "I thirst" (John 19:28)? Do you think he observed the ribaldry and scorn that surrounded the dying Lord? Did he feel that the stones would cry out if he did not show kindness to his best friend? Since Jesus spoke not for Himself but was dumb as a sheep before her shearers, Joseph is bound to open his mouth for Him. If Jesus answered not but only breathed out prayers for His murderers, the honorable counselor must acknowledge Him. The sun has owned Him and veiled its face in sackcloth! The earth has owned Him and trembled to its very heart at His sufferings! Death has owned Him and yielded up the bodies that the sepulcher had hitherto detained! The temple has owned Him and in its horror has rent its veil like a woman that is utterly broken in heart by the horrors she has seen! Therefore Joseph must own Him, He cannot resist the impulse. Oh, brethren and sisters, if you have been backward, let some such motive lead you to the van of the host.

Then there were all *the wonders of that death* which he saw, and to which I have already alluded. They sufficed to convince the centurion that this was a righteous man. They convinced others that He was the Son of God, and he who was already a disciple of Christ must have been greatly confirmed in that conviction by what he saw around the cross. The time was come when he must boldly act as Christ's disciple. Have there been no wonders of conversion around you? No answers to prayer? No providential deliverances? Should not these lead the secret ones to declare themselves?

I do not suppose he fully understood *the design of our Lord's death.* He had some knowledge of it but not such a knowledge as we have now that the Spirit of God has appeared in all His fullness and taught us the meaning of the Cross. Oh, listen, you that are not upon His side openly, you that have never worn His livery nor manifestly entered on His service. He died for you! Those wounds were all for you. That bloody sweat, of which you still may see the marks upon the countenance of the Crucified, was all for you: for you the thirst and fever, for you the bowing of the head and the giving up of the ghost. Can you be ashamed to own Him? Will you not endure rebuke and scorn for His dear sake who bore all this for you? Now speak from your soul and say, "He loved me and gave Himself for me." If you cannot say that, you cannot be happy. But if you can, then what follows? Must you not love Him and give yourself for Him? The Cross is a wondrous magnet, drawing to Jesus every man of the true metal. It is as a banner lifted on high to which all who are loyal must rally. This fiery Cross, carried through all lands, will rouse the valiant and speed them to the field. Can you see your Lord suffering to the death for you and then turn your backs? I pray you may no longer hesitate but may at once cry, Set down my name among His followers. For I will fight it out even to the end, until I hear Him say,

> Come in, come in;
> Eternal glory thou shalt win.

Thus much by way of instruction is taken from the life of Joseph of Arimathea. If the Cross does not bring a man out, what will? If the spectacle of dying love does not quicken us into courageous affection for Him, what can?

Our Arousing

Perhaps you are saying in your heart that the season in which Joseph lived was one that imperatively demanded that he should leave his hiding place and should go in to Pilate but that you are under no such constraint. Hearken, friends, many people are not true to their occasions, whatever they may be. They do not consider that they have come to the kingdom for such a time as this. The Lord Jesus is not hanging on a cross today needing to be buried, but other stern necessities exist and call for your exertions. This hour's necessities imperiously demand that every man who is right at heart should acknowledge his Lord and do Him service. Every man that loves Christ should at this hour prove it by his actions. A buoy off the Mumbles in South Wales bears a bell which is meant to warn mariners of a dangerous rock. This bell is quiet enough in ordinary weather. But when the winds are out and the great waves rush in toward the shore, its solemn tones are heard for miles around as it swings to and fro in the hands of the sea. I believe there are true men who are silent when everything is calm who will be forced to speak when the wild winds are out. Permit me to assure you that a storm is raging now, and it is growing worse and worse. If I rightly read the signs of the times, it is meet that every bell should ring out its warning note lest souls be lost upon the rocks of error. You that have fallen behind because the fighting did not seem to require you must quit your positions of ease. I summon you in the Master's name to the war. The Lord has need of you. If you come not to His help against the mighty a curse will light upon you. You must either be written across the back as craven cowards, or else you will today solemnly espouse the cause of Jesus. Shall I tell you why?

I will tell you why Joseph was wanted, and that was just because *Christ's enemies had at last gone too far.* When they hunted Him about and took up stones to stone Him, they went a very long way. When they said He had a devil and was mad, they went much too far. When they asserted that He cast out devils by Beelzebub, the prince of the devils, that was a piece of blasphemy. But now, now they have overstepped the line most fatally. They have actually taken the King of Israel and nailed Him up to a cross, and He is dead. Therefore Joseph cannot stand it any longer. He quits their company and joins himself to the Lord Jesus.

See how far men are going in these days. In the outside world we have infidelity of so gross, so brutish a character that it is unworthy of the civilization, much less of the Christianity, of our age. Now, fearful ones, come out and refuse to be numbered with the unbelieving world. Besides, in the outward Christian church we see men who, having already taken away every doctrine that we hold dear, are now assailing the inspiration of God's own Word. They tell us plainly that they do not believe what the Scriptures say further than they choose to do. The Bible, to them, is a fine book but rather out of date. Now, if you can be quiet, I cannot. The citadel of Christendom is now attacked. Let no brave man shrink from its defense. If you can hold your tongues and see the faith rent to pieces, I cannot. Why, it is enough to make every man gird on his weapon and rush to the fight.

Years ago, when they talked of the French invading England, an old lady grew very indignant and threatened deadly resistance. When she was asked what the women of England could do, she said they would rise to a man. I have no doubt whatever that they would do their best in any such emergency. Every iron in the fireplace, whether it be poker or shovel, would be grasped to defend our hearths and homes. Just so now, when error knows no bounds, we must stand up for the defense of the truth. Since they push error to extremes, it becomes us to hold by every particle of the faith. I will not, for my own part, give up a corner of my creed for any man. Even if we might have been prepared to modify expressions had the age been different, we are not in that mood now. A generation of vipers shall have a naked file to bite at. We will modify nothing. If truth bears a stern aspect, we will not veil it. If there be an offense in the Cross, we will not conceal it. This shall be my answer to those who would have us attune ourselves to the spirit of the age— I know no Spirit but one, and He is unchanging in every age. Your extravagance of doubt shall have no influence over us except to make us bind the Gospel more closely to our hearts. If we gave you an inch, you would take a mile, and so no inch shall be given you. Our resolve is to live for the Book as we read it, for the Gospel as we rest in it, for the Lord as He made atonement, for the kingdom as it rules over all. I beg every trembling Christian to take heart, put on his Lord's livery, and advance to the fray. Come out now, if you never did before! Come out, if there is any manliness in you in these days of blasphemy and rebuke.

> Ye that are men, now serve Him
> Against unnumber'd foes;
> Your courage rise with danger
> And strength to strength oppose.

When Joseph of Arimathea revealed himself as our Lord's disciple, *our Lord's friends had mostly fled*—we might almost say they had all departed. Then Joseph said, "I will go in and beg for the body." When everybody else runs away, then the timid man grows brave. Often have I noticed that when there has been a wide desertion from the faith, then the feeble have become strong. Those poor souls who had said, "We hardly know whether we are the people of God at all we are so unworthy," have crept out of their dens and have waxed valiant in fight, putting to flight the armies of the aliens. A sister was asked to tell her experience before the church, and she could not do it. But as she went away she turned around and said, "I cannot speak for Christ, but I could die for Him." "Come back," said the minister, "you are welcome here!" They do gloriously, those hidden ones, in days whereof we are apt to fear that no witness for the truth will remain alive. Oh, that you who live where religion is declining may be all the more resolved to serve the Lord Jesus faithfully!

And then, you know, in Joseph's time *the people that were true to the Lord Jesus were such a feeble company.* Those that were not absolutely poor—the women that could minister to Him of their substance—were nevertheless unable to go in to Pilate and beg for the Lord's body. He would not have received them, and if he would they were too timid to have sought an interview. But Joseph is rich and a counselor, and therefore he seemed to say, "These dear good women need a friend. They cannot get that precious body down from the cross alone. I will go to the Roman governor. Together with Nicodemus, I will provide the linen and the spices. The women shall help us take Jesus down from the tree and lay Him in my new tomb and swathe His limbs in linen and spices, so as to embalm Him honorably." Some of you live in country towns where those who are faithful to God are very poor and have not much ability among them. If anything should move you to be the more decided, it should be that fact. It is a brave thing to help a feeble company. Any common people will follow at the heels of success, but the true man is not ashamed of a despised cause when it is the cause of truth. You who have talent and substance should say, "I will go and help them now. I cannot leave the Master's cause to this feeble folk. I know they do their best, and as that is little, I will join them and lay myself out to aid them for my great Master's sake."

Can you not see my drift? My only desire this morning is to induce any of you who have for a moment faltered to "stand up, stand up for Jesus" and everywhere, in every place as wisdom may suggest, avow His clear and sacred name. Perhaps you are flowers that cannot bloom until the light is darkened, like the night-blooming cereus or the evening primrose. Now is your hour. The evening is already come. Bloom, my dear friends, and fill the air with the delightful fragrance of your love. When other flowers are closed, take care to open to the dew. In these dark hours shine out, you stars! The sun has gone, else might you lie hid, but now let us see you! Joseph and Nicodemus had never been seen in the daylight when Jesus was alive. But when the sun was set through His death, then their radiance beamed at its full. Oh, my hesitating friend, now is your time and your hour. Boldly avail yourself of it, for our great Master's sake!

Our Guidance

Somebody says, "Well, what do you mean by my coming out? I can see what Joseph did. What am I to do? I do not live at Arimathea, and there is no Pilate in these days."

Joseph in owning his Lord *put himself under personal risk.* A Christian slave, whose master was executed for being a Christian, went to the judge and begged the body of his master that he might bury it. The judge replied, "Wherefore do you wish for your master's body?" "Because he was a Christian, and I am one." Upon this confession he was himself condemned to die. It might have been so with Pilate, for the Jewish rulers must have hated Joseph and longed for his death. He had been backward a long time, but now he put his life in his hands and went in boldly to Pilate. We read, "He craved the body of Jesus." But, as a commentator well says, he was not a craven, though he craved the body. He simply asked for it, begged for it, implored to have it, and the procurator yielded to his wish. Now, do you think that if it were needful for you to jeopardize your best earthly interests for Christ, you could do it? Could you lose your character for culture and courage by avowing the old faith in these apostate days? Can you leave all for Jesus? Should it rend the fondest connection, should it break up the brightest prospects, could you take up the cross and follow your Lord? It is due to Him who died for you that you should count the cost and reckon it little enough for His dear sake if you may but do Him honor.

Remember, again, that this good man, Joseph of Arimathea, when he took the body of Jesus brought upon himself *ceremonial pollution.* It may seem little enough to you, but to a Jew it was a great deal, especially during the Passover week. He handled that blessed body and defiled himself in the judgment of the Jews. But, oh, I warrant you he did not think it any defilement to touch the blessed person of his Lord, even when the life was gone out of that matchless frame, nor was it any pollution. It was an honor to touch that holy thing, that body prepared of God. Yet they will say to you that, if you come out for Christ and unite with His people, you lower yourself. They will point at you, give you some opprobrious name, and charge you with fanaticism. Take upon yourself this blessed shame and say, as David did, "I will yet be more vile" (2 Sam. 6:22). Dishonor for Christ is honor, and shame for Him is the very top of all glory. You will not stand back, I trust, but you will come forward and avow your faith though you thus become as the offscouring of all things.

And then, this man, having risked his life and given up his honor, was content to be *at great cost for the burial of Christ.* He went and bought the fine linen, and that rock-hewn sepulcher, which it was the ambition of every Israelite to possess, he cheerfully resigned that the Lord might lie there. Now, whenever you do own Christ, own Him practically. Do not keep back your purse from Him or think that you are to say, "I am His," and do nothing for Him. I was reading the story of a good old deacon in Maine, America, who came into a meeting after there had been a missionary collection. The minister there and then asked "our good brother Sewell" to pray. Sewell did not pray, but thrust his hand in his pocket and stood fumbling about. "Bring the box," he said. When the box came and he had put his money into it, the minister said, "Brother Sewell, I did not ask you to give anything, I only wished you to pray." "Oh," said he, "I could not pray until I had first given something." He felt obliged first to do something for the great mission work, and having done that he could pray for it. Oh, that all Christ's people felt the justice of that course of conduct! Is it not most natural and proper? Joseph could not, when the Savior wanted burying, have been true to Him without burying Him. And now that the Savior does not want burying but wants in all His living power to be preached among the sons of men, if we love Him we must do all that lies in us to spread the knowledge of His name.

Come out then, come out then, you that are hidden among the stuff! Some of you strangers from the country who have lived in the village and attended the services but never joined the church, do not let another Sunday dawn until you have sent in your name to be classed with the people of God. And any of you that have come often to the Tabernacle and say that nobody has spoken to you, just you speak to somebody and own what the Lord has done for you. Joseph of Arimathea, where are you? Come forward, man! Come forth; your time has come! Come forth now! If you have followed Christ secretly, throw secrecy to the winds! Henceforth be bravest of the brave among the bodyguard of Christ who follow Him whithersoever He goes. Have no fear nor thought of fear, but count it all joy if you fall into manifold trials for His name's sake, who is King of Kings and Lord of Lords, to whom be glory forever and ever. Amen.

7

Peter's Restoration

And immediately, while he yet spake, the cock crew. And the Lord turned, and looked upon Peter. And Peter remembered the word of the Lord, how he had said unto him, Before the cock crow, thou shalt deny me thrice. And Peter went out, and wept bitterly (Luke 22:60–62).

Peter had terribly fallen. He had denied his Master, denied Him repeatedly, denied Him with oaths, denied Him in His presence while his Master was being smitten and falsely charged. He had denied Him, though he was an apostle, denied Him, though he had declared that should all men forsake Him, yet would he never be offended. It was a sad, sad sin. Remember what led up to it. It was, first, Peter's presumption and self-confidence. He reckoned that he could never stumble and for that very reason he speedily fell. A haughty spirit goes before a fall. Oh, that we might look to the roots of bitter flowers and destroy them! If presumption is flourishing in our hearts today, we shall soon see the evil fruit that will come of it. Reliance upon our firmness of character, depth of experience, clearness of insight, or matureness in grace will, in the end, land us in disgraceful failure. We must either deny ourselves, or we shall deny our Lord. If we cleave to self-confidence, we shall not cleave to Him.

Immediately, Peter's denial was owing to cowardice. The brave Peter in the presence of a maid was ashamed. He could not bear to be pointed out as a follower of the Galilean. He did not know what might follow upon it. But he saw his Lord without a friend and felt that it was a lost cause, and he did not care to avow it. Only to think that Peter, under temporary discouragement, should play the coward! Yet cowardice treads upon the heels of boasting. He that thinks he can fight the world will be the first man to run away.

This sermon was taken from *The Metropolitan Tabernacle Pulpit* and was preached on Sunday morning, July 22, 1888.

His sin also arose from his want of watchfulness. His Master had said to him, "What, could ye not watch with me one hour?" (Matt. 26:40) and no doubt there was more meaning in the words than appeared on the surface. The Lord several times said to him, "Pray, that ye enter not into temptation" (v. 41). The words were repeated with deep impressiveness, for they were greatly needed. But Peter had not watched; he had been warming his hands. He did not pray; he felt too strong in himself to be driven to special prayer. Therefore, when the gusts of temptation came, they found Peter's boat unprepared for the storm, and they drove it upon a rock.

When Peter first denied his Master a cock crowed. Peter must have heard that crowing or he would not have communicated the fact to the Evangelists who recorded it. But though he heard it, he was an example of those who have ears but hear not. One would have thought that the warning would have touched his conscience, but it did not. When the cock crowed a second time, after he had committed three denials, it might not have awakened him from his dreadful sleep if a higher instrumentality had not been used, namely, a look from the Lord Jesus.

God keep us free from this spirit of slumber, for it is to the last degree dangerous! Peter was under the direful influence of Satan, for it was a night wherein the powers of darkness were specially active. "This is your hour," said Jesus, "and the power of darkness." (Luke 22:53). That same influence which assailed the Savior unsuccessfully—for, said He, "the prince of this world cometh, and hath nothing in me" (John 14:30)—assailed Peter with sad result, for the Evil One had something in Peter, and he soon found it out. The sparks from Satan's flint and steel fell upon our Lord as upon water. But Peter's heart was like a tinder box, and when the sparks fell, they found fuel there. Oh, that we may be kept from the assaults of Satan! "Lead us not into temptation" is a necessary prayer, and the next petition is specially noteworthy, "but deliver us from the evil one" (Matt. 6:13). A man never gets anything out of the Devil, even if he conquers him. You will find in combat with him that, even if you win the victory, you come off with gashes and wounds of which you will carry the scars to your grave. "All the while," says Mr. Bunyan, while Christian was fighting with Apollyon, "I did note that he did not so much as give one smile." Oh, no! there is nothing to smile about when the Archenemy is upon us. He is such a master of the cruel art of soul wounding that every stroke tells. He knows our weak places in the present, he brings to remembrance our errors in the past, and he paints in blackest colors the miseries of the future and so seeks to destroy our faith. All his darts are fiery ones. It takes all a man's strength, and a great deal more, to ward off his cunning and cruel cuts. The worst of it is that, as in Peter's case, he casts a spell over men so that they do not fight at all but yield themselves an easy prey. Our Savior said to Peter, "Simon, Simon, behold, Satan hath desired to have you, that he may sift you as wheat: but I have prayed for thee, that thy faith fail not" (Luke 22:31–32). Peter was as much under the power of Satan as corn is in the hand of the man who winnows it. He went up and down in that sieve like a helpless thing and so passed from simple falsehood to plain denials of his Master with oaths and cursings.

I desire in this discourse to speak chiefly of Peter's restoration. Peter was down, but he was soon up again. One writer says the story should rather be called Peter's restoration than Peter's fall. His fall was soon over. He was like a little child learning to walk, scarcely down before his mother has him up again. It was not a continuance in a sin, like David who remained for months without repentance. But it was the quick speech of a man carried away by sudden temptation, and it was followed by a speedy repentance. Upon his restoration we are going to meditate.

It was brought about by two outward means. I like to think of the singular combination: the crowing of the cock and a look from the Lord. When I come to preach to you, it almost makes me smile to think that God should save a soul through me. I may find a fit image of myself in the poor cock. Mine is poor crowing. But as the Master's look went with the cock's crowing, so, I trust, it will go with my feeble preaching. The next time you also go out to try and win a soul for Jesus, say to yourself, "I cannot do it. I cannot melt a hard, rebellious heart, yet the Lord may use me. If there come a happy conjunction of my feeble words with my Lord's potent look, then the heart will dissolve in streams of repentance." Crow away, poor bird. If Jesus looks while you are crowing, you will not crow in vain, but Peter's heart will break. The two things are joined together, and let no man put them asunder—the commonplace instrumentality and the divine Worker. Christ has all the glory and all the more glory because He works by humble means. I trust that there will be this morning a conjunction of the weakness of the preacher with the strength of the Holy Spirit, so that stony hearts may be broken and God glorified.

This morning, first, *let us look at the Lord who looked*; secondly, *let us look into the look that the Lord looked*; and then, thirdly, *let us look at Peter upon whom the Lord looked*. We will be all the while looking; may our Lord look upon us. May His Holy Spirit work with His holy Word!

The Lord Who Looked upon Peter

Can you picture the Lord up there in the hall, up yonder steps, before the high priest and the council? Peter is down below in the area of the house warming his hands at the fire. Can you see the Lord Jesus turning around and fixing His eyes intently upon His erring disciple? What do you see in that look?

I see in that look, first, that which makes me exclaim: *What thoughtful love!* Jesus is bound, is accused, has just been smitten on the face, but His thought is of wandering Peter. You want all your wits about you when you are before cruel judges and are called upon to answer false charges. You are the more tried when there is no man to stand by you or to bear witness on your behalf. It is natural, at such an hour, that all your thoughts should be engaged with your own cares and sorrows. It would have been no reproach had the thoughts of our Lord been concentrated on His personal sufferings; all the less so because these were for the sake of others. But our blessed Master is thinking of Peter, and His heart is going out toward His unworthy disciple. That same influence that made His heart drive out its store of blood through every pore of His body in the bloody sweat now acted upon His soul and drove His thoughts outward toward that member of His mystical body who was most in danger. Peter was thought of when the Redeemer was standing to be mocked and reviled. Blessed be His dear name, Jesus always has an eye for His people, whether He be in His shame or in His glory. Jesus always has an eye for those for whom He shed His blood. Though now He reigns in glory, He still looks steadily upon His own. His delight is in them, and His care is over them. There was not a particle of selfishness about our Savior. "He saved others; himself he cannot save" (Matt. 27:42; Mark 15:31). He looked to others, but He never looked to Himself. I see, then, in our Lord's looking upon Peter a wondrously thoughtful love.

I exclaim, next: *What boundless condescension!* If our Lord's eye had wandered that day upon "that other disciple" that was known to the high priest, or if He had even looked upon some of the servants of the house, we should not have been so astonished. But when Jesus turns, it is to look upon Peter, the man from whom we should naturally have turned away our faces after his wretched conduct. He had acted most shamefully and cruelly, and yet the Master's eye sought him out in boundless pity! If there is a man here who feels himself to be near akin to the Devil, I pray the Lord to look first at him. If you feel as if you had sinned yourself out of the pale of humanity by having cast off all good things and by having denied the Lord that bought you, yet still consider the amazing mercy of the Lord. If you are one of His, His pitying eye will find you out. For even now it follows you as it did Hagar when she cried, "Thou God seest me" (Gen. 16:13). But oh, the compassion of that look! When first I understood that the Lord looked on me with love in the midst of my sin, it did seem so wonderful! He whom the heavens adore, before whose sight the whole universe is stretched out as on a map, passes by all the glories of heaven that He may fix His tender gaze upon a wandering sheep and may in great mercy bring it back again to the fold. For the Lord of glory to look upon a disciple who denies Him is boundless condescension!

And then, again: *What tender wisdom!* "The Lord turned, and looked upon Peter." He knew best what to do. He did not speak to him but looked upon him. He had spoken to Peter before, and His voice had called him to be a fisher of men. He had given Peter His hand before and saved him from a watery grave when he was beginning to sink. But this time He gives him neither His voice nor His hand but that which was equally effectual and intensely suitable: He lent him His eye. The Lord looked upon Peter. How wisely does Christ always choose the way of expressing His affection and working our good! If He had spoken to Peter then, the mob would have assailed him, or at least the ribald crowd would have remarked upon the sorrow of the Master and the treachery of the disciple. Our gracious Lord will never needlessly expose the faults of His chosen. Possibly no words could have expressed all that was thrown into that look of compassion. Why, friends, a volume as big as a Bible is contained within that look of Jesus. I defy all the tongues and all the pens in the world to tell us all that our divine Lord meant by that look. Our Savior employed the most prudent, the most comprehensive, the most useful method of speaking to the heart of His erring follower. He looked volumes into him. His glance was a divine hieroglyphic full of unutterable meanings that it conveyed in a more clear and vivid way than words could have done.

As I think of that look again, I am compelled to cry out: *What divine power!* Why, dear friends, this look worked wonders. I sometimes preach with all my soul to Peter, and, alas! he likes my sermon and forgets it. I have known Peter to read a good book full of most powerful pleading, and when he has read it through, he has shut it up and gone to sleep. I remember my Peter when he lost his wife. One would have thought it would have touched him, and it did with some natural feeling. Yet he did not return to the Lord whom he had forsaken but continued in his backsliding. See, then, how our Lord can do with a look what we cannot do with a sermon, what the most powerful writer cannot do with hundreds of pages, and what affliction cannot do with even its heaviest stroke. The Lord looked, and Peter wept bitterly. I cannot help thinking with Isaac Williams that there is a majestic simplicity in the expressions here used:—"The Lord turned, and looked upon Peter. . . . And Peter went out, and wept bitterly." The passage reminds us of that first of Genesis: "And God said, Let there be light: and there was light." As the Lord looked to the host of the Egyptians and troubled the Egyptians, so did He now look into Peter's heart, and his thoughts troubled him. Oh, the power of the Lord Christ! If there was this power about Him when He was bound before His accusers, what is His power now that He is able to save to the uttermost them that come to God by Him, seeing He ever lives to make intercession for them? In that look there was divinity. The Son of God looked upon Peter. The text does not use the name Jesus, but it expressly says, "The Lord turned, and looked upon Peter." That divine look did the deed.

Let me beg you to note: *What sacred teaching!* The teaching is of practical value and should be at once carried out by the followers of Jesus. You, dear friend, are a Christian man or a Christian woman. You have been kept, by divine grace, from anything like disgraceful sin. Thank God it is so. I dare say, if you look within, you will find much to be ashamed of, yet you have been kept from presumptuous and open sins. Alas! one who was once a friend of yours has disgraced himself. He was a little while ago a member of the church, but he has shamefully turned aside. You cannot excuse his sin. On the contrary, you are forced to feel great indignation against his folly, his untruthfulness, his wickedness. He has caused the enemies of the Lord to blaspheme and has done awful mischief to the cause of righteousness. Now I know what will be suggested to you. You will be inclined to cut his acquaintance, to disown him altogether, and scarcely to look at him if you meet him in the street. This is the manner of men but not the manner of Jesus. I charge you, act not in so un-Christlike a manner. The Lord turned and looked on Peter; will not His servants look on him? You are not perfect like your Lord. You are only a poor, sinful creature like your fallen brother. What? are you too proud to look at the fallen one? Will you not give him a helping hand? Will you not try to bring him back? The worst thing you can do with a backslider is to let him keep on sliding back. Your duty should be your pleasure, and your duty is to "restore such an one in the spirit of meekness; considering thyself, lest thou also be tempted" (Gal. 6:1). O brothers and sisters, it is a very little thing that has kept some of us from turning aside to folly. One grain more and the scale would have turned in favor of a great fall. Our steps have well-nigh slipped. When we are proud of our sure standing, the Lord may well be angry with us for our vanity. He may justly say, "How can I endure this pride? I have taken great care of this man and watched over him to keep him out of sin. Now he takes the credit of it all, plays the great man, and fancies that he will be defiled if he associates with my poor wandering children." Which, think you, is worse in God's sight, the sudden fall into sin or the long-continued pride that boasts itself in the presence of the Lord and looks contemptuously upon erring ones? It is not my office to become a measurer of sins. But I would earnestly enforce this plain duty: Since our own Lord and Master looked on backsliding Peter, let us seek out our wandering brethren.

One more lesson: *What heavenly comfort!* "The Lord turned, and looked upon Peter"; yes, Jesus looks upon sinners still. The doctrine of God's omniscience is far more often set forth in a hard way than in a cheering way. Have you never heard a sermon from "Thou God seest me" of which the pith was: Therefore tremble and be afraid? That is hardly fair to the text. When Hagar cried, "Thou God seest me," it was because the Lord had interposed to help her when she had fled from her mistress. It was comfort to her that there she also had looked after Him that had looked upon her. There is a dark side to "Thou God seest me." But it is not half so dark as it would be if God did not see us. It is true, O sinner, that God has seen your sin and all the aggravations of it. But it is also true that as He sees your ruin, your misery, your sadness, He has compassion on you. He sees your sin that He may remove it and make you clean in His sight. As the Lord looked upon Peter, so He looks upon you. He has not turned His back on you; He has not averted the gaze of His pity. He sees to the bottom of your heart and reads all your thoughts. You have not to go about to find out God—He is looking upon you. "He [is] not far from every one of us" (Acts 17:27). He is within eyesight. You are to look to Him. If you do, your eyes will meet His eyes, for already He looks upon you.

I think we have gathered much from this brief look at the Lord who looked upon Peter. I doubt not that, had we more time and more insight, we should see greater things than these.

The Look the Lord Gave Peter

Let us look into the look that the Lord gave Peter. That look was, first of all, *a marvelous refreshment to Peter's memory.* "The Lord turned, and looked upon Peter." What a sight it must have been for Peter! Our dear Master's face was that night all red from the bloody sweat. He must have appeared emaciated in body, His eyes weary with want of sleep, and His whole countenance the vision of grief. If ever a picture of the Man of Sorrows could have been drawn, it should have been taken at that moment when the Lord turned and looked upon Peter. By torchlight and the flickering flame of the fire in the court of the hall of Caiaphas, Peter saw a vision that would never fade from his mind. He saw the man whom he loved as he had never seen Him before. This was He who called him, when he was fishing, to become a fisher of men. This was He who bade him spread the net and caused him to take an incredible quantity of fishes insomuch that the boat began to sink, and he cried out, "Depart from me; for I am a sinful man, O Lord" (Luke 5:8). This was He who had made him walk on the water and at other times had rebuked the winds and raised the dead. This was He with whom Peter had been upon the Mount of Transfiguration! Truly there was a wonderful change from the glistening whiteness of the mount to the ghastliness of that sad hour! Though the lineaments of that reverend face were stained with blood, yet Peter could tell that it was the selfsame Lord with whom he had enjoyed three years of close relationship and tender unveiling. All this must in a moment have flashed upon poor Peter's mind. I do not wonder that in the recollection of it all he went out and wept bitterly. He did love his Lord. His denial was not of the heart but of the tongue. Therefore, as all the grounds of his faith came before his mind anew, his heart was broken into a thousand pieces with grief that he should have been false to such a friend. Yes, that look awoke a thousand slumbering memories, and all these called upon the sincere heart of Peter to repent of its ungenerous weakness.

Next, that turning of the Master was *a special reminder of His warning words*. Jesus did not say it in words, but He did more than say it by His look. "Ah, Peter! did not I tell you it would be so? You said, 'Though all men shall be offended because of thee, yet will I never be offended' (Matt. 26:33). Did I not tell you that before cock-crowing you would deny me thrice?" No rebuke was uttered, yet the tender eye of the Lord had revealed to Peter his own extreme folly and his Master's superior wisdom. Now he saw his own character and perceived his Lord's discernment. It was a prophecy, and, like all other prophecies, it was understood after it was fulfilled. We read that "Peter remembered the word of the Lord, how he had said unto him, Before the cock crow, thou shalt deny me thrice." It is clear, then, that our Lord's look was a special reminder of His former words. It stirred up Peter's mind by way of remembrance and made him see how foolish he had been and how inexcusable was his fault.

Surely it was, also, *a moving appeal to Peter's heart*. I bade you notice just now, in the reading of the chapter, that this story of Peter is singularly interwoven into the narrative of our Savior's passion. It is so interwoven because it constitutes an essential part of that passion. We must not regard it as an accidental incident; it was part and parcel of that grief that He had to bear when He stood in our place and stead. It was written of old, "Smite the shepherd, and the sheep shall be scattered" (Zech. 13:7). This scattering of the sheep, of which Peter was a notable instance, was one of the bitter ingredients of our Redeemer's mental anguish. "Lover and friend hast thou put far from me" (Ps. 88:18) is His complaint in the psalm. When the Savior showed Himself to Peter with all those lines of grief upon His face, He seemed to say to him, "Can you deny Me now? I am bound for you, and do you deny Me? I stand here to be adjudged to death for you, and do you deny Me? Now is the hour of my agony, and do you deny Me?" The Lord could not have looked at Peter without creating strong emotion in the breast of the weak disciple who now found himself in so sad a plight. That look touched very tender cords. There was no need for a single word of appeal. That look sufficed to stir the deeps of Peter's nature.

What do you think that look chiefly said? My thought about it, as I turned it over, was this: When the Lord looked upon Peter, though He did refresh his memory and make an appeal to his conscience, yet there was still more evidently *a glorious manifestation of love.* If I may be permitted humbly and reverently to read what was written on my Master's face, I think it was this: "And yet I love you, Peter, I love you still! You have denied Me, but I look upon you still as Mine. I cannot give you up. I have loved you with an everlasting love, and, notwithstanding all your ill conduct toward Me, I am looking for you and expecting to receive you. I have not turned My back on you. Behold, I look toward you with tender regard, foreseeing that you will yet serve Me and prove the truth of your devotion to Me. Despair not, O Peter, for I will receive you again, and you shall glorify Me." Judging what would break my heart the soonest if I had thus denied my Master, it seems to me that I should be most affected by His saying to me, "And yet, despite your sin, I love you still." Love is the great heartbreaker.

Immutable love is that divine hammer that breaks the rock in pieces. Though a man should have sinned himself into great hardness of heart, yet almighty love can soften him. Who can resist the charms of grace unchangeable? Sharper than a sword is a look of love; more fierce than coals of juniper are the flames of love. One said, the other day, speaking of a person who has gone awfully astray after having been a preacher of the Word, "If I did not believe in the doctrine of unchanging love I do not think I dare pray for him. But since I believe that God will bring him back again, I pray with humble confidence that he will be restored." That which is an encouragement to prayer for others will be a help toward our return if we have gone astray. I love to believe that my Lord will bring His wanderers back. O you who are anxious to return to Him, let this cheer you: "Yet doth he devise means, that his banished be not expelled from him" (2 Sam. 14:14). This doctrine wins men back. There are wicked men who turn it into an argument for continuing in sin; their damnation is just. True men will see, in the measureless and unchanging love of Christ, a reason that will put wings to their feet when they hasten back to Him from whom they have gone astray.

Again: this look *penetrated Peter's inmost heart.* It is not every look that we receive that goes very deep. I look with eyes of deep affection at men from this pulpit and perceive that they know my meaning, but they soon shake it off. But our Savior has an eye to which the joints and marrow are visible. He looks into the secret chambers of the soul, for His look is a sunbeam and bears its own light with it, lighting up the dark places of our nature by its own radiance. Peter could not help feeling, for he was pricked in the heart by the arrow of Christ's glance. How many persons are affected by religion only in the head! It does not affect their hearts and lives. I am grieved when I hear of some of you who are regular hearers and take pleasure in my preaching; yet, after many years, you are not a bit better. You have had spasms of improvement, but they have ended in nothing. You go back to the mire after you have been washed. You are a hearer of the Gospel and yet a drunkard. Your voice is heard in a psalm, but it may also be heard in an oath. It is a shocking thing, but I have done my best. I can preach to your ears, but I cannot look into your hearts. Oh, that my Lord would give such a glance at you this morning as should dart light into you and cause you to see yourself and to see Him. Then the tears would fill your eyes!

One fact may not escape our notice: Our Lord's look at Peter was *a revival of all Peter's looking to Jesus*. The Lord's look upon Peter took effect because Peter was looking to the Lord. Do you catch it? If the Lord had turned and looked on Peter and Peter's back had been turned on the Lord, that look would not have reached Peter nor affected him. The eyes met to produce the desired result. Notwithstanding all Peter's wanderings, he was anxious about his Lord and therefore looked to see what was done with Him. Even while he warmed his hands at the fire, he kept looking into the inner hall. His eyes were constantly looking in the direction of the Lord Jesus. While he wandered about among the maids and serving men and got talking to them—fool that he was—still he would perpetually steal a glance that way to see how it fared with the man he loved. He had not given up the habit of looking to his Lord. If he had not still, in a measure, looked to his Master, how would the look of Jesus have been observed by him? His eye must look through your eye to get to your heart. The remainders of faith are the sparks among the ashes of piety, and the Lord blows on these to raise a fire. If there is a poor soul here that despite his backsliding can yet feel, "I am trusting in Jesus, and if I perish, I will perish there," there is hope for that soul. If you have given up the outward forms of religion it is a grievous fault. But if you still inwardly look to the Crucified, there is something in you to work upon, there is an eye that can receive the look of Jesus. It is through the eye that looks to Jesus that Jesus looks and lets fresh light and hope into the soul. Oh, that you who have this lingering faith in the Lord may now receive a look from Him that shall work in you a bitter, salutary, saving repentance without which you can never be restored!

This look was *altogether between the Lord and Peter*. Nobody knew that the Lord looked on Peter except Peter and his Lord. That grace that saves a soul is not a noisy thing, neither is it visible to any but the receiver. This morning, if the grace of God comes to any one of you in power, it will be unperceived by those who sit on either side of you in the pew. They will hear the same words, but of the divine operation that accompanies them they will know nothing. The eye of the Lord will not speak to them as it is speaking to the awakened one. Do you know anything of the secret love-look of the Lord Jesus?

The whole process may not have occupied more than a second of time. The Lord turned and looked on Peter. It took less time to do than it takes to tell. Yet in that instant an endless work was done. How soon can Jesus change the heart! "He spake, and it was done." I venture to alter that verse and say, "He looked, and it was done." Lord, look on sinful Peter now! Work a miracle with Your eye! Even here, let some sinner look to You because You have looked on him.

Peter after the Lord Had Looked at Him

What is Peter doing? When the Lord looked on Peter *the first thing Peter did was to feel awakened.* Peter's mind had been sleeping. The charcoal fire had not done him much good, the fumes of it are evil. The dust of Satan's sieve had gotten into his eyes. He was confused with very sorrow for his dear Master, whom he truly loved. Peter was hardly Peter that night. I think I had better say, Peter was too much Peter, and his mind had more of Peter's stone in it than of Christ's flesh. He had forgotten that he was an apostle. He had forgotten that which he had declared when the Lord said to him, "Blessed art thou, Simon Bar-jona: for flesh and blood hath not revealed it unto thee" (Matt. 16:17). Again, I remind you how significantly it is written, *"The Lord* turned, and looked upon Peter," for it hints that Peter now saw his Lord's deity through the veil of His humiliation and anguish. He had forgotten his Lord's deity, and thus he had, in thought, denied his Lord. He was off the lines and was in a sleepy state. He was what Paul calls "bewitched" and under the influence of a spiritual soporific administered by Satan. The Lord's look brought him to his better self and aroused all the spiritual life that had been dormant in him. "Peter remembered," and by this remembrance he was restored.

The next effect was *it took away all Peter's foolhardiness from him.* Peter had made his way into the high priest's hall, but now he made his way out of it. He had not felt in any danger though in the worst of company. What did he care for the girl that kept the door? Surely he was too much of a man to mind her remarks. What did he care for the men that were around the fire? They were rough fellows, but he had been a fisherman and quite able to cope with the priest's bailiffs. But now the brag is gone out of him. No sooner had Jesus looked upon him than Peter declined all further risks.

Now he shows the better part of valor and with great discretion quits the dangerous society of the high priest's palace. Revival of grace in the heart is the death of presumption. The man who runs risks with his soul is not in a right state of mind. Perhaps the Savior's glance conveyed a hint to Peter that he had no business where he was. It may have seemed to say to him, "You had better be gone from these surroundings." At any rate, that was the effect it produced. That palace in which the Lord fared so badly could not be a fit place for a disciple. To be warming himself at the fire was quite inconsistent for Peter while Jesus was being mocked of His enemies. A sight of the Lord Jesus makes many things seem incongruous that else might appear right enough. All Peter's daring vanished. He turned his back on maids and men and went out into the darkness of the night. We do not hear of his coming near the cross. In fact, we hear no more of him until the resurrection morning, for Peter was sensible enough to feel that he could not trust himself anymore. He placed himself in the background until his Lord summoned him to the front. I wish that some religious professors whose lives have been questionable had grace enough to do the same. When I see a man who has sinned grievously pushing himself speedily to the front, I cannot believe that he has a due sense of the evil he has wrought or of his own unfitness to be in the place of peril.

Above all, shun the place where you have fallen. Do not linger in it for a moment. Go out even though you leave the comfortable fire behind you. Better be in the cold than stay where your soul is in danger. Until Peter had received from the Lord's own mouth abundant assurance of his restoration to his office by the threefold charge to feed the sheep and lambs, we do not find him again in the forefront.

That look of Christ severed Peter from the crowd. He was no longer among the fellows around the fire. He had not another word to say to them. He quitted their company in haste. It is well for believers to feel that they are not of the world! They should flee out of Sodom. The Lord has severed us from the multitude by His divine choice and the separation should be our choice.

Oh, that the arrows of the great Lord would this morning pierce some soul even as a huntsman wounds a stag! Oh, that the wounded soul, like Peter, would seek solitude! The stag seeks the thicket to bleed and die alone, but the Lord will come in secret to the wounded heart and draw out the arrow. Alone is the place for a penitent. Out in the darkness is far better for you than around the fire where coarse jokes are bandied while Christ is mocked. There must be confession and weeping alone. If Christ has looked upon you, you must get away from the men of the world and indeed from all others. The solitude of your chamber will suit you best.

That look of Christ also opened the sluices of Peter's heart. He went out and wept bitterly. There was gall in the tears he wept, for they were the washings of his bitter sorrow. Dear friends, if we have sinned with Peter, God grant us grace to weep with Peter. Many will think of Peter's wandering who forget Peter's weeping. Sin, even though it be forgiven, is a bitter thing. Even though Christ may look away your despair, He will not look away your penitence. "He went out, and wept bitterly." Oh, how he chided himself! "How could I have acted so!" How he smote on his breast and sighed, "How can I ever look up? Yet is He very precious. That look forgave me, but I can never forgive myself." He remembered it all his life and could never hear a cock crow without feeling the water in his eyes.

Yet I want you to notice that *that look of Christ gave him relief.* It is a good thing to be able to weep. Those who cannot weep are the people that suffer most. A pent-up sorrow is a terrible sorrow. The Lord touched a secret spring and made Peter's grief flow out in floods, and that must have greatly eased him. I have frequently heard people say, "I had a good cry, and after that, I was able to bear it." People die of bursting hearts when no tears relieve them. I thank God for Peter that he could weep bitterly, for thus the Holy Spirit came to him with comfort. O Master, look on some poor, dry heart here—some poor heart that cannot feel its sinfulness, but would if it could—and give it feeling! Look on the heart that cannot repent, that is crying, "I would, but I cannot feel contrition." Lord, you made the rock yield water at the smiting of the rod; use Your poor stick of a servant this morning to smite the rocky heart, and let the waters of repentance flow out.

And now, to conclude, *it made Peter, as long as he lived, ashamed to be ashamed.* Peter was never ashamed after this. Who was it that stood up at Pentecost and preached? Was it not Peter? Was he not always foremost in testifying to his Lord and Master? I trust that if any of us have been falling back, and especially if we have wandered into sin, we may get such a restoration from the Lord Himself that we may become better Christians ever afterward. I do not want you to break a bone, I pray God you never may. But if you ever do, may the heavenly Surgeon so set it that it may become thicker and stronger than before. Courage was the bone in Peter that snapped. But when it was set, it became the strongest bone in his nature and never broke again. When the Lord sets the bones of His people, they never break anymore—He does His work so effectually. The man who has erred by anger becomes meek and gentle. The man who has erred by drink quits the deadly cup and loathes it. The man who has sinned by shame becomes the bravest of the company.

O Lord Jesus, I have tried to preach You this morning, but I cannot look with Your eye. You must look on erring ones Yourself. Look, Savior! Look, sinner! "There is life in a look at the crucified One," because there is life in a look *from* the crucified One. May Jesus look, and may the sinner look! Amen.

8

Peter after His Restoration

When thou art converted, strengthen thy brethren (Luke 22:32).

Peter was to be sifted, so our Lord warned him, and Satan was to operate with the sieve. Satan had an intense desire to destroy Peter—indeed, he would like to destroy all the chosen of God— and therefore he desired to sift him as wheat in the hope that he would be blown away with the husks and the chaff. To see a child of God perish would bring to the Evil One a malicious joy, for he would have wounded the heart of God. If ever the fallen spirit can be happy, he would derive happiness from defeating the grace of God and robbing the Lord Jesus of those whom He bought with His blood. "Satan hath desired to have you" (v. 31). It would be a satisfaction to him to have a believer in his power. He was anxious to get Peter into his clutches to give him as tremendous a shaking as he could manage.

If Satan knows, as he no doubt does, concerning any one believer that he cannot quite destroy him, then he is especially anxious to worry him. If he cannot devour the chosen, he would at least defile them. If he cannot ruin their souls, he would break their quiet. As the Revised Version puts it, Satan even asks of God to have them that he may sift them as wheat. This is a curious statement, for it seems from it that the Devil can pray and that his petition may be granted him. The margin has it, "Satan hath obtained you by asking." The Lord may grant the request of the Devil himself, and yet He would not prove thereby that He had any love toward him. The Lord's wisdom may grant Satan's desire and in the very act overthrow his evil power. Let us not then stake our faith in the Lord's love upon His giving us the precise answer we desire. For what He gives to Satan He may see fit to deny to those whom He loves, and He may do so because He loves them.

This sermon was taken from *The Metropolitan Tabernacle Pulpit* and was preached at the Metropolitan Tabernacle, Newington.

It is a fact that the Evil One is permitted to test the precious metal of God's treasury. The story in the Book of Job is no fiction or piece of imagination. It is even so that Satan desires to have choice ones of God put into his power that he may test them—that he may torment them, that he may, if possible, destroy them. The Lord may permit this, as He did in the case of Job and as He did in the case of the apostles and specially in the case of Peter. He may grant the Tempter's request and allow him to touch our bone and our flesh and see whether we will hold to our God in mortal agony.

We are not bound to know God's reasons for what He does or permits. It is sometimes sinful to inquire into those reasons. What the Lord does is right; let that be enough for us who are His children. But we can see sometimes a reason why the saints should be sifted as wheat, for it appertains to wheat to be sifted because it is wheat. Sifting brings a desirable result with it. It is for the saints' good that they should be tried. Satan doubtless wishes that he may let the good seed fall to the ground and be destroyed. But God overrules it to separate the chaff from the wheat and to make the wheat into clean grain fit for storage in the King's granary. Satan has often done us a good turn when he has meant to do us a bad one. After all, he is only a scullion in God's kitchen to clean His vessels. Some of them have received special scouring by means of his harsh temptations.

God also may find a reason for allowing His saints to be tempted of Satan, and that reason may have more relation to others than to themselves. They may have to be tested for other people's good. The testing of their faith is "more precious than of gold that perisheth, though it be tried with fire" (1 Peter 1:7), and part of its preciousness is its usefulness. The child of God under temptation behaving himself grandly will become a standing example to those who are around him. "Ye have heard of the patience of Job" (James 5:11); but you never would have heard of the patience of Job if Satan had not sifted him. This great treasury of instruction, the Book of Job, and all the truth taught us by Job's example comes to us through God's having permitted Satan to put forth his hand and to press the patriarch so sorely. We also may be afflicted not so much for ourselves as for others. This may be remarkably the case in the instances of those of you whom God makes useful to a large circle of friends. You live for others and therefore suffer for others. The whole of your lives will not be accounted for by you yourselves but by your surroundings. As a minister I may have to be tempted because temptation is one of the best books in a minister's library. As a parent you may need affliction because a father without a trial can give no counsel to a tempted child. Public workers may have to be tried in ways that, to a private Christian, are unnecessary. Let us accept remarkable discipline if thereby we are qualified for remarkable service. If by the roughness of our own road we are trained to conduct the Lord's sheep along their difficult pathway to the pastures on the hilltops of glory, let us rejoice in every difficulty of the way. If apostles and men like Peter had to be put into Satan's sieve while they were being trained for their lifework, we may not hope to escape.

Observe, dear friends, what came before the sifting and went with the sifting. Note well that blessed "but." "But I have prayed for thee," not, Thy brethren have prayed for thee; not, Thou hast prayed for thyself. But, "I have prayed for thee." Jesus, that master in the art of prayer, that mighty pleader who is our advocate above, assures us that He has already prayed for us. "I have prayed for thee" means before the temptation I have prayed for you. I foresaw all the danger in which you would be placed, and concerning that danger I have exercised My function as High Priest and Intercessor. "I have prayed for thee." What a divine comfort is this to any who are passing through deep waters! You only go where Jesus has gone before you with His intercession. Jesus has made provision for all your future in a prayer already presented: "I have prayed for thee." You may be much comforted by the prayers of a minister or of some Christian man who has power with God, but what are all such intercessions compared with the praying of your Lord? It were well to have Noah, Samuel, and Moses praying for us, but better far to have Jesus say, "I have prayed for thee." Blessed be God, Satan may have his sieve, but as long as Jesus wears His breastplate we shall not be destroyed by Satan's tossings.

Notice that the principal object of the prayer of our Lord was "that thy faith fail not." He knows where the vital point lies, and there He holds the shield. As long as the Christian's faith is safe the Christian's self is safe. I may compare faith to the head of the warrior. O Lord, You have covered my head in the day of battle for You have prayed for me that my faith fail not. I may compare faith to the heart, and the Lord holds His shield over the heart that we may not be injured where a wound would be fatal. "I have prayed for thee, that thy faith fail not." Faith is the standard-bearer in every spiritual conflict; if the standard-bearer fall, then it is an evil day. Therefore our Lord prays that the standard-bearer may never fail to hold up his banner in the midst of the fray: "I have prayed for thee, that thy faith fail not." If faith fails, everything fails: courage fails, patience fails, hope fails, love fails, joy fails. Faith is the root grace; if this be not in order, then the leafage of the soul, which shows itself in the form of other graces, will soon begin to wither. "I have prayed for thee, that thy faith fail not."

Learn a lesson from this, my friend—that you take care to commend your faith to your God. Do not begin to doubt because you are tempted—that is to lay bare your breast. Do not doubt because you are attacked—that is to loosen your harness. Believe still. "I had fainted," said David, "unless I had believed" (Ps. 27:13). It must be one thing or the other with us. Believing or fainting, which shall it be? "Above all, taking the shield of faith" (Eph. 6:16), not only take it so that it may cover all, but make this the vital point of holy carefulness. Watch in all things, but specially guard your faith. If you be careful about one thing more than another, above all be careful of your faith. "I have prayed for thee, that thy faith fail not." Our Savior's pleading goes to the point, and thus it teaches us where to direct our own desires and our own prayers. He asks for us far more wisely than we shall ever learn to ask for ourselves. Let us copy His petitions.

Therefore it follows because of Christ's prayer that, though Peter may be very badly put to it, yet he shall be recovered, for Christ speaks of it as of an assured fact—"When thou art converted," as much as to say, When you come back to your old life and your old faith, then exercise yourself usefully for your Lord. He speaks of Peter's restoration as if it were quite sure to be. And is it not quite sure to be? If Jesus, the Beloved of the Father, prays for His people, shall He not win His suit with God? He will win it! He will uplift Peter from among the siftings where Satan has thrown him. We are sure He will, for in prospect thereof, He sets him a loving and suitable task: "When thou art converted, strengthen thy brethren." The establishment and confirmation of all the rest are to hinge upon the setting up in his place of poor, thrice-denying Peter.

Now, beloved friends, I may be addressing a number of persons who believe on the Lord Jesus Christ as Peter did, but they have fallen into a bad state and need a new conversion. I am very sorry for you, but I am by no means staggered at the sight of you, for you belong to a numerous class. When sitting to see inquirers I am constantly stumbling on backsliders who come back very sincerely and very truly and feel right pleased to find a Christian home again. I meet with many who have been outside in the world, some of them for years, attending the house of God very irregularly and seldom or never enjoying the light of God's countenance. They have wandered so that none can tell whether they are the Lord's or not, except the Lord Himself, and He always knows them that are His. I bear happy witness that the Lord brings His own back again. Though the Lord's sheep stray, yet the Good Shepherd finds them. Though the Lord's children go into the far country, yet they each one in due time say, "I will arise, and go to my Father" (Luke 15:18). It is not every prodigal that returns, but only the prodigal *son*. In due time, the son returns to the Father's house. It is not every bit of stuff that falls on the ground that is found again, but the woman's piece of money is sure to be discovered. She will not lose it. It is hers, and she values it. She sweeps the house and makes any quantity of dust until she finds it. The Lord will find His own, even though Satan tries to prevent the gracious discovery.

It may be some of you have wandered into error. May you be brought back very speedily. If you are, we are going to say to you tonight, "Strengthen your brethren." Possibly there has been a general decay in grace within your soul. You have lost your joy, your peace, your love, your zeal. This is sad; may the Lord restore you in answer to the prayer of Him that redeemed you. Then, when you are converted, seek to recover your brethren from the decay of their graces that has also injured them. You will not be converted in quite the same sense as you were at first, but you will be turned again to your old life and hope. Then you are to strengthen your brethren by aiming at their restoration to their first love and earliest zeal.

Perhaps you have been neglectful. I find that many who were good Christian people in the country, always at the house of prayer and walking near to God, will come up to this wicked London to live, and the change is a serious injury to them. They get lost to Christian society, and by degrees they become deteriorated by the ungodliness of this modern Sodom. Nobody in the street wherein they live ever goes to a place of worship. They do not know anybody at the chapel or at the church, so they give up going to public worship and fall into the ways and habits of the ungodly world. They are not happy. God's children never are happy when they leave their Father. If you have ever eaten the white bread of heaven, you will never rest content with the black ashes of earth. If the flavor of Christ's love has once been in your mouth, you are spoiled for a worldling. You will not make an expert sinner now, for your hand is out of it. Once converted, you must be a child of God or nothing. You are ruined for this world. If the world to come is not yours, where are you? The Devil himself will not like you long. You are not of his sort. There is a something about you that will not suit Satan any more than Jonah suited the whale. The whale was quite as glad to part with Jonah as Jonah was to be set free from the whale.

I see arrangements for your coming home again. The Lord devises means that His banished shall not perish. Those tokens of disquiet, those startings in your sleep, those horrible forebodings, those inward hungerings are all pulling at you to come home. You have been trying to feed upon the dust that is ordained to be the serpent's meat, and if the Lord had not loved you, you would have done so. A deceived heart has turned you aside, but in love to your soul the Lord has made you aware of it, and your cry is, "I will go and return to my first husband; for then was it better with me than now" (Hos. 2:7). These are tokens by which I am assured that the Lord will bring His own back. I rest confident that He will turn them, and they shall be turned. I am going to talk to backsliders about what they are to do when they do come back again.

We are going to take it for granted that they will come back and to speak to them now about what it is their privilege to attempt under such gracious circumstances. "When thou art converted, strengthen thy brethren." First, *it is the restored man's duty;* secondly, *he has a special qualification for it;* and thirdly, *it will be a great blessing to him to set about it.*

The Restored One's Duty

He has gone astray, and he has been brought back. What better can he do than to strengthen his brethren? *He will thus help to undo the evil that he has wrought.* Peter must have staggered his brethren. Some of them must have been quite frightened at him. John soon looked after him, but then they were not all Johns. Full of love, John soon hunted up Peter, but the others must have felt that he was a mere reed shaken by the wind. It must have staggered the faith of the weaker sort to see that Peter, who had been such a leader among them, was among the first to deny his Lord. Therefore, Peter, you must build what you have thrown down and bind up what you have torn! Go and talk to these people again, and tell them how foolish and weak you were. Warn them not to imitate your example. You must henceforth be more bold than anybody else that you may in some measure undo the mischief that you have done.

Now, do think of this, any of you who have been cold toward the Lord. You have wasted months, even years, in backsliding. Try to recover lost ground. It will be almost impossible for you to do it, but do at least make a serious attempt. If anybody has been staggered by your backsliding, look after him, try to bring him back and strengthen him. Ask his pardon and beg him to recover the strength of which you helped to rob him. This is the least that you can do. If almighty love has drawn you back again after sad wanderings, lay yourself out with all your heart to do good to those who may have been harmed by your sad turnings aside. Am I asking more of you than simple justice demands?

Besides, *how can you better express your gratitude to God* than by seeking to strengthen your weak brethren when you have been strengthened yourself? After our first conversion, you and I were found seeking earnestly after sinners like ourselves. We had been newly brought out of the house of bondage, and we longed to lead other slaves into the liberty wherewith Christ makes men free. This, I say, we ought to do when first brought to Jesus' feet. But if to our disgrace we have turned aside and have backslidden, and if to God's infinite glory He has restored our souls and made us strong again, then we ought to renew our zeal for the salvation of others. We ought to have a special eye to backsliders like ourselves. We should say, "Lord, I will show how much I thank You for restoring me by endeavoring to find any that have been overtaken in a fault that I may restore such in the spirit of meekness, remembering myself also, since I have been tempted and have not stood against the temptation." Those of you whom the Good Shepherd has restored should have a quick eye for all the sickly ones of the flock and watch over these with a sympathetic care. You should say, "This is the field that I shall try to cultivate. Because in my spiritual sickness the Lord has been pleased to deal so graciously with me, I would therefore lay myself out to cherish others who are diseased in soul."

Do you not think, too, that this becomes our duty because, *doubtless, it is a part of the divine design?* Never let us make a mistake by imagining that God's grace is given to a man simply with an eye to himself. Grace neither begins with man nor ends with him with an object confined to the man's own self. When God chose His ancient people Israel, it was not merely that Israel might enjoy the light, but that Israel might preserve the light for the rest of the nations. When God saved you, He did not save you for your own sake but for His own name's sake, that He might through you show forth His mercy to others. We are windows through which the light of heavenly knowledge is to shine upon multitudes of eyes. The light is not for the windows themselves but for those to whom it comes through the windows. Have you ever thought enough about this? When the Lord brings any of you back from your backsliding, it is decidedly with this view—that you may be qualified to sympathize with others and wisely guide them back to the fold. All your history, if you read it aright, has a bearing upon your usefulness to your fellowman. If you have been permitted in an hour of weakness to grow cold or turn aside, and if the Lord in unspeakable compassion has restored you to His ways, surely this must be His motive—that you may afterward strengthen your brethren.

By the way, the very wording of the text seems to suggest the duty: we are to strengthen our "brethren." We must do so in order that we may manifest brotherly love and thus prove our sonship toward God. Oh, what a blessed thing it is when we come back to God and feel that we are still in the family! That was the point which we debated with ourselves. We feared that we were not the Lord's.

> 'Tis a point I long to know,
> Oft it causes anxious thought.

Whatever some may say about that hymn, I do not give much for the man who has not sometimes had to sing it in the minor key. It is a pity that he ever should have to sing it. He will not if he walks before the

Lord with care and watchfulness. But when he has been a naughty child, when his life has not been what it should be, if he does not doubt himself we must take leave to doubt for him. How can he help asking,

> Do I love the Lord or no?
> Am I his or am I not?

I am inclined to say with a good experimental writer,

> He that never doubted of his state,
> He may—perhaps he may too late.

It is not an ill thing to try yourselves and see whether your faith is gold or dross. To have a question about your position in the heavenly family is a very painful thing and should not be endured one moment if it be in your power to solve the doubt. But if the Lord has brought you back as His child, you now know that you belong to the family, and it will be suggested at once to you to do something for the brethren. Naturally, you will look around to see whether there be any child of God to whom you can show favor for his Father's sake. You have injured all by your backsliding; hence it is your duty when restored to the family to benefit them all by special consecration and double earnestness. Let it be your delight, as well as your duty, to strengthen your brethren. Prove that you are a brother by acting a brother's part. Claim your privilege as a child and exercise it as a child should by helping another child that is in need. I think that the text within itself contains this argument.

Let us see to it, dear friends, if we have been restored that we try to look after our weak brethren *that we may show forth a zeal for the honor and glory of our Lord.* When we went astray we dishonored Christ. If any of these others go astray they will do the same. Therefore let us be watchful that if we can we may prevent their being as foolish as we have been. Let us learn tenderness from our own experience and feel a deep concern for our brethren. If one member of this church sins we all suffer—in our reputation, at any rate. Especially, the best known among us have to bear a great deal because of the inconsistency of this person and of that. Do you want us to be wounded through you? My beloved friends, I do not think that one of you would wish to cast reproach upon your minister. Alas! Christ Himself suffers. His worst wounds are those that He receives in the house of His friends. Peter, if you ever denied your Master, mind you look well to others who are growing presumptuous as you were before your great sin. If you meet anyone who is beginning to say, "I will go with you to prison and to death," give him a gentle jog and say, "Mind, brother; you are going near a nasty hole into which I once fell. I pray you take warning from me." If you speak experimentally, you will have no cause to boast, but you will find in your own sin a reason why you should tenderly guard your brethren lest they should cause like dishonor to that dear name that is more precious, I hope, to you than life itself. "When thou art converted, strengthen thy brethren." It is your duty.

The Restored One Has a Qualification for It

This Peter is the man who, when he is brought back again, can strengthen his brethren. He can strengthen them by telling them of *the bitterness of denying his Master.* He went out and wept bitterly. It is one thing to weep; it is another thing to weep bitterly. There are sweet tears, as well as salt tears, but oh, what weeping a sin costs a child of God! I recollect a minister speaking very unguardedly. He said that the child of God lost nothing by sin except his comfort. I thought, "Oh, dear me! And is that nothing? Is that nothing?" It is such a loss of comfort that, if that were all, it would be the most awful thing in the world. The more God loves you and the more you love God, the more expensive will you find it to sin. An ordinary sinner sins cheaply; the child of God sins very dearly. If you be the king's favorite, you must mind your manners for he will not take from you what he will take from an enemy. The Lord your God is a jealous God because He is a loving God. He has such love for His own chosen that if they turn aside His jealousy burns like coals of juniper. May God keep us from ever provoking His sacred jealousy by wandering at any time into any kind of sin. Now Peter, because he could tell of the bitterness of backsliding, was the man to go and speak to anyone who was about to backslide and say, "Do not so, my brother, for it will cost you dearly."

Again, Peter was the man to tell another of *the weakness of the flesh* for he could say to him, "Do not trust yourself. Do not talk about never going aside. Remember how I talked about it. I used to be very lofty in my talk and in my feelings, but I had to come down. I felt so sure that I loved my Lord and Master that I put great confidence in myself and could not think that I should ever wander from Him. But see, see how I fell. I denied Him thrice before the time called cock-crowing." Thus, you see, Peter was wonderfully qualified by having known the bitterness of sin and by feeling the weakness of his own flesh to go and strengthen others in these important points.

But he was also qualified to bear his personal witness to *the power of his Lord's prayer.* He could never forget that Jesus had said to him, "I have prayed for thee." He would say to any brother who had grown cold or presumptuous, "The Lord Jesus prayed for me. It was because of His prayer that I was preserved from going farther so that I was led back and delivered from the sieve of the Evil One." Do you not think that this

would strengthen any trembling one when Peter mentioned it? It is wonderful how men and women are helped by those who have had a similar
experience to theirs. Theory is all very well, but to speak experimentally
has a singular power about it. How one can comfort the bereaved if one
has been bereaved oneself! But how little can the young and inexperi-
enced yield of consolation to those who are greatly tried, even though
they are anxious to do so! And so, brethren, if the Lord has blessed you
and remembered you in His great mercy, and if you know the power of
the prayer of the great Intercessor, you can strengthen your brethren by
reminding them of the perseverance of the Savior's love.

And could not Peter speak about *the love of Jesus to poor wanderers?*
The Lord turned and looked upon Peter, and that look broke Peter's heart.
Afterward the Lord spoke to Peter by the sea and said to him, "Feed my
lambs. . . . Feed my sheep" (John 21:16–17). O beloved, Peter would always remember that, and he would speak of it to any whom he found in a
sad and weary condition. He would say, "My Lord was very good to me
and was willing to receive me back. No, He did not wait until I came
back, but He came after me. He sent after me, saying, Go tell My disciples and Peter. When He saw that I was penitent, He never rebuked me,
except in such a gentle sideway that I was rather comforted than rebuked
by what He said." Oh, you that have wandered and Christ has restored
you, comfort the wanderers when you see their tears! When you hear any
word of doubt or anything like despair from them, tell them that there is
no truth in the suggestion of Satan that Christ is unwilling to forgive.
Beseech them not to slander that dear heart of love which is infinitely
more ready to melt toward the penitent than the penitent's heart is to melt
toward it. You knew it. You know that you can speak not only what you
have read in the Bible, but what you have felt in your own heart. You are
qualified, therefore, to strengthen your brethren.

And could not Peter fully describe *the joy of restoration?* "Oh," he
would say, "do not wander. There is no good in it. Do not go away from
Jesus. There is no profit to be found there. Come back to Him. There is
such peace, such rest with Him. Never, never go away again." Peter ever
afterward in his epistles—and we are sure that it must have been the
same in his spoken ministry—testified to the love and goodness of
Christ and urged the saints to steadfastness in the faith. I would appeal to
any child of God here whether he ever gained anything by going away
from Christ. No, brothers and sisters, the old proverb says that honesty is
the best policy. But I will turn it to a higher use and say, holiness is the
best policy. Communion with Christ is the happiest life. If you gained all
the world, and did not lose your soul but only lost the light of Christ's
countenance for a few days, you would make a poor bargain. There is
heaven in every glance of His eye. There is infinite joy in every word of

His mouth when He speaks comfortably to His servants. Go not away from Him. Be like Milton's angel who lived in the sun. Abide in Christ and let His words abide in you. Closer, closer, closer, this is the way to spiritual wealth. To follow afar off and live at a distance from Christ, even if it does not make your soul to perish, yet it will wither up your joys and make you feel an unhappy man, an unhappy woman. Therefore, all those who have tried it should bear their witness and put their experience into the scale as they thus strengthen their brethren.

It Will Be Such a Benefit to the Restored One

The restored one will derive great personal benefit from endeavoring to cherish and assist the weak ones in the family of God. Brother and sister, do this continually and heartily, for thus *you will be made to see your own weakness.* You will see it in those whom you succor. As you see how they doubt or grow cold or become lukewarm, you will say to yourself, "These are men of like passions with me. I see which way I shall drift unless the grace of God sustains me." It will lead you to throw out another anchor and get a fresh hold as you see how they yield to the tide. One man is wonderfully like another man, only that other men are better than we are. When we are trying to strengthen them, we are not to look upon ourselves as superior beings but rather as inferior beings and say, "He fell yesterday, I may fall today. If I do not fall today, I may tomorrow." All the weaknesses and follies you see in others, believe that they are in you yourself and that will tend to humble you. I think that a true minister is often excited to better work by what he sees of weakness in his people because he says to himself, "Am I feeding this flock well?" Perhaps he thinks to himself, "If I had properly tended them they would not have shown all these weaknesses." Then he will begin to blame his own ministry and look to his own heart, and that is a good thing for us all. We very seldom, I think, blame ourselves too much, and it is a benefit to us to see our own failings in others.

But what *a comfort* it must have been to Peter *to have such a charge committed to him!* How sure he must have felt that Jesus had forgiven him and restored him to His confidence when the Lord, having asked him, "Lovest thou me?" said to him, "Feed my lambs. . . . Feed my sheep." Peter is all right again or else Christ would not trust lambs to him. Peter must be all right or else Jesus would not put the sheep under his care. It is a grand proof of our being fully restored to the divine heart when the Lord entrusts us with work to do for His own dear children. If you and I are made the means of strengthening our brethren, what a comfort it will be to our hearts! I know that it is not the highest form of comfort, for Jesus would say of it, "In this rejoice not, . . . but rather rejoice, because your names are written in heaven" (Luke

10:20). But still to a loving child of God it is no mean consolation to find that God is using him. I know, for my own part, that when I go to see our friends who are ill and near to die, it is a supreme consolation to see how calm they always are, without any exception, yes, and how joyful they generally are—how triumphant in the departing hour! Then I say to myself, "Yes, my Master has owned my ministry." The seals of fresh conversions are very precious, but the surest seals are these dying saints who have been nurtured in the Gospel that we have preached. They prove the truth of it, for if they do not flinch when they stand looking into eternity but even rejoice in the prospect of meeting their Lord, then what we preach is true, and our Master has not left us without witness. So you see that it is a great benefit to a man to strengthen his brethren because it becomes a comfort to his own soul.

And, brethren, whenever any of you lay yourselves out to strengthen weak Christians, as I pray you may, *you will get benefit from what you do in the holy effort.* Suppose you pray with them. Well, then, you will pray a little more than if you only prayed for yourself, and anything that adds to your prayerfulness is a clear gain. I wish that you had the habit of making everybody pray with you that comes to your house, saying to them, "Now we have done our little business, let us have a word or two of prayer." Some even of God's people would look at you. It will do them good to look at you and learn from you the blessed habit. With regard to those who are strangers to divine things there will often occur opportunities in which you have put them under an obligation, or they have come to you in trouble to ask advice, and then you may boldly say, "Do not let us part until we have prayed." We used to have an old member of this church who used to pray in very extraordinary places. Two women were fighting and he knelt down between them to pray, and they gave over fighting directly. Before a door when there has been a noise in the house he has begun to pray. He was better than a policeman, for his prayer awed the most obstinate. They could not understand it. They thought it a strange thing, and they did not care to put themselves into direct opposition to the man of God. There is a wonderful power in prayer to bless us ourselves, besides the blessings that it will bring upon others. Pray with the weak ones, and you will not be a weak one yourself.

Then, think of your example. If you use your example to strengthen the weak—if you carefully say to yourself, "No, I shall not do that because, though I may do it, I may do injury to some weak one"—this will do you good. If you hesitate, if you draw back from your own rights and say, "No, no, no; I am thinking of the weak ones"—you will get good from that self-denial. If the poor, trembling, wandering backslider is much upon your mind, you will often be very tender how you act. You will look to see where your foot is going down next time, for fear of treading upon somebody or other. In that way you will be winning for yourself the great gain of a holy carefulness of walk and conversation—no small gain to you.

And again, suppose that in trying to strengthen these weak ones, you begin to quote Scripture to them—quote a promise to them—this will bless you. Some of you do not know which promise to quote. You do not even know where to find it in the Word. But if you are in the habit of studying Scripture with a view to strengthening the weak, you will understand it in the best way, for you will get it in a practical form and shape. You will have the Bible at your fingers' ends. Moreover, one of these days the text that you looked out for old Mary will suit yourself. How often have we paid Paul with that which we meant to give to Peter! We have ourselves fed on the milk we prepared for the babes. Sometimes what we have laid up for another comes in handy for ourselves. We strangely find that we ourselves have been fed while we were feeding others, according to that promise, "He that watereth shall be watered also himself" (Prov. 11:25).

Now, I have said all this to you that have wandered and come back, and I want to say it right home to you. May the Holy Spirit speak to your inmost souls. You know who you are and how far all this applies to you. The Lord bless you.

But, dear friends, if you have not wandered, if the Lord has kept you these twenty years close to Him and given you the light of His countenance all that time, then I think that you and I, and any of us of that sort, ought to strengthen our brethren still more. Oh, what we owe to sovereign grace! To be kept from wandering—what a blessing is that! Let us feel that instead of having a small debt to pay, we have a greater debt to acknowledge. Let us wake up to strengthen our brethren. I ask this of you, members of the church, because in so large a church as this unless there is a kind of universal mutual pastorate, what can we do? You that are converted, I beseech you to strengthen your brethren.

And then, if all this ought to be done to those who are in the family, what ought we not to do for those outside—for these that have no Christ and no Savior? If you are converted yourself, seek the salvation of your children, of your own brothers and sisters, and of all your household. Try to bring in your neighbors to hear the Word. Get them, if you can, under the sound of the Gospel. Why should we not fill up on Thursday night until the uppermost gallery is full? There are some friends up there tonight, and I am glad to see them. May God bless them. I hope that the day will come when every seat will be occupied there so that when we are preaching the Gospel we may scatter it broadcast and find a field upward as well as downward where the seed may fall. Oh, for a blessing! May we meet in heaven to praise the Lord our God. Amen.

9

Stephen and Saul

*And cast him out of the city, and stoned him: and the witnesses laid
down their clothes at a young man's feet, whose name was Saul
(Acts 7:58).*

The Holy Spirit does not tell us much about the deaths of saints at
any time, and He says very little about the deaths of the martyrs.
He gives us much more about Stephen—the first of them—than
about any other. A few words are made to suffice for the death of
James, the brother of John. As to the deaths of Peter and Paul, they are
incidentally mentioned as yet to be, but we have no account of them
whatever. I suppose there was no need, and the Holy Spirit never gives
us superfluous information. There were hundreds of years to come in
which martyrologies might be written. The Lord has taken care that
there should be eyewitnesses with ready pens to record the deaths of
martyrs. Hence we have many volumes, and especially in our own
country, the renowned *Acts and Monuments* of John Foxe, that record
how through seas of blood the martyrs swam to their crowns. The noble
army of martyrs has never been without a chronicler. There was no
need that the Holy Spirit should give us the details of the deaths of the
witnesses for Christ because we should have plenty in another form.

And it is noteworthy that in this one, which is the fullest we have,
there is nothing said about the sufferings of Stephen. Have you not had
your feelings harrowed by descriptions of the burnings in the reign of
Queen Mary—how the torches were slowly lighted; how, sometimes,
the martyrs actually cried out, "For pity's sake, give us more fire"; how
they writhed in agony and yet cried out, "None but Jesus"? Such details
may be very proper, but I think that they minister to our sentiment
rather than to our edification. The Holy Spirit takes a different line and

---

This sermon was taken from *The Metropolitan Tabernacle Pulpit* and was
preached on Thursday evening, May 13, 1875.

tells of the triumph of the martyr, of the light that shone upon his face, of the vision that he beheld that cheered his spirit, and of the blessed calm that came over him as Jesus rose up and rebuked the winds and waves that gathered round his barque so that the martyr entered into the port of peace in a perfect calm. I believe that every incident that is recorded is intended for our profit. It is not always profitable to have sensational descriptions that harrow one's feelings. There is something better than that, namely, to teach us the true source of strength and to guide us to a heavenly calm, come what may.

However, in this instance, the Holy Spirit was pleased to direct the pen of Luke to record that the witnesses laid down their clothes at the feet of a young man named Saul. According to the Jewish law, the witnesses were bound to be the first throwers of the stones. They were, in fact, the leading executioners, for they gave evidence against the accused, and on their witness he was condemned to death. They had to take the responsibility of his death and to throw the first stones. In order to do this, they took off their long, flowing robes, and, casting them down, they left them in the charge of one who would appear to have been much delighted with the death of Stephen. He had probably given his vote against him in the Sanhedrim and was looking on to see that the dreadful murder was fully accomplished. Now, why is it recorded that these witnesses laid down their clothes at the feet of the young man whose name was Saul? It was not to gratify our curiosity, but it was doubtless for some good reason. So let us try to find out why it is recorded and learn some lessons from it, God helping us.

A Very Noteworthy Contrast

Here are two men—Stephen and Saul—both in heaven now. I wonder how they felt when they first met there! What joy they must both have had—Stephen to see Saul and Saul to see Stephen! I suppose it is incompatible with the heavenly state for Saul to have any apologies to make. But, certainly, if they could have been indulged in there, he might have made them most lovingly and tenderly. The joy of meeting there must have been exceedingly great. Look at the two men—the one about to die and the other taking care of the clothes of the executioners. Let us do them justice.

They were both sincere men. There was no hypocrisy about Stephen. You could see that the words that he spoke came warm from his heart. Neither was there any hypocrisy about Saul. He really thought that he was doing God service in what he did. He was quite as sincere, in his own way, as was the martyr who was about to die. What is more, *they were both thoroughly earnest men.* It was not in the nature of Stephen to quench his convictions or to silence his testimony. Neither was it in the nature of Saul to keep quiet when he thought that a miserable impostor ought to be crushed out of existence. He is all on fire from the first moment when we meet with him to the last record we have concerning him. He had a zeal for God, though not according to knowledge. As he sat there and took care of the executioners' garments, he felt in his conscience perfectly satisfied that what he was doing was for the glory of God. Sometimes we cannot understand how this could be. Yet I do not doubt that many who have persecuted the saints of God have done it ignorantly in unbelief, and it has not struck them that they were really rebelling against the Most High and fighting against the Lord Himself. It is very difficult to estimate the amount of darkness that may come over the human conscience and to imagine how blind a man may become or how fully he may put bitter for sweet and sweet for bitter. But certain it is that an unrenewed heart may become so darkened that while we are going posthaste to hell we may imagine that we are making good headway toward heaven. These two men, Stephen and Saul, were unlike one another in many respects, but they were alike in this sense, that they were both sincere and both thoroughgoing in their sincerity.

But, now, observe the difference between them. *Look first at Saul, a man wrapped up in self-righteousness.* He will tell you that he has kept the commandments from his youth up. If you gave him time, he would, perhaps, tell you that by descent he was a Hebrew of the Hebrews— that, as touching the law, he was blameless—that he belonged to the straightest sect of his religion and was a Pharisee. If you began to charge him with sin, you would see the fire flash from his eyes as he declared that, concerning the righteousness that was by the law, he was without fault. If any man was accepted before God, he felt that he was. There he sat, in all the pride of self-righteousness, assisting at the murder of a truly righteous man.

Had you spoken to Stephen, you would have found a man of quite another class. *The martyr's only hope was in the crucified Christ of Calvary.* That which gladdened him was not a sight of himself but a sight of his exalted Lord. He drew his comfort not from what he had done but from the finished work of Him who was, at that moment, standing at the right hand of the Father.

What a difference there was between those two men! Perhaps there may be two such persons here sitting very near each other: the one self-righteous and self-reliant, depending only upon his own good works; the other, humbly looking away from self and trusting only to the Lord Jesus Christ for salvation. Of you two, I would sooner be you who are looking to Christ, even though you are to be executed tonight, than I would be you, sir, who are wrapped up in the robes of your fancied self-righteousness, even though you are honored and respected by all mankind.

Look again at Saul and you will see *a man ritualistic to the utmost extent—a formalist of the deepest dye.* He is a man who highly esteems everything that has to do with the temple, the priesthood, and the law. You will find that his phylacteries are exceedingly broad. If you speak to him about the sacred roll of the Old Testament, you will find that he can debate and discuss with you upon every letter of it, for he has a great attachment to the letter. He is a man entirely taken up by the externals of religion. The shell is everything to him.

But now look at Stephen, and you will see a man who has put external matters altogether on one side. That last speech of his shows that it is so. He has not despised the temple, but he has said of it, "Howbeit the most High dwelleth not in temples made with hands" (v. 48). He has not despised the chosen people, Israel, but he has spoken of them as "stiffnecked and uncircumcised in heart and ears" (v. 57). He has not despised the outward forms of religion so far as they were ordained of God. But he has shown that in themselves they are useless because, even when they were in the full tide of their glory, they did not change men's hearts, for many remained idolaters and murmurers in the wilderness. Stephen is the spiritual man, and Saul is the formal man.

Both these classes may be represented here. I would have you see to which of them you belong because it is the spiritual worshiper whom God seeks. It is the spiritual worshiper who is God's friend, but the formalist is no friend of the King of heaven, though he may seem to be so. He fights for the letter of the Word, but, in despising its inner meaning, he has despised the very essence of it. He fights for rites and ceremonies, but, in neglecting the inward and spiritual grace, he has neglected the vital matter. He remains as much a foe of God and of His Christ as was this young man named Saul.

The great difference between Stephen and Saul, however, lies in this: *Stephen is defending the cause of Christ at the cost of his own life, and Saul is opposing him with all his might.* Even in a congregation like the present, there may not be many, yet there may be some who are opposing the Gospel. There may be some here who, although they would not stone believers, yet would make a jest of them. Perhaps they have been making merry today over those Christian brethren who have of late been prominent in the matter of revivals—some foolish jest they have perpetrated about them and done their best to lower them in the esteem of their fellows. Ah, dear friends, beware what you are at, for the Lord of Hosts says concerning His people that "He that toucheth you toucheth the apple of his eye" (Zech. 2:8). Nothing brings the color into a man's cheek sooner than any ill-treatment of his children. If any of you want to provoke God to speedy and sudden judgment against you, you have only to join in treating in a cruel manner those who really are His children. May God keep all of us from such a shameful sin as that!

The contrast mentioned in our text is a very painful one, and though we see it illustrated every day, it is nonetheless painful. We ought to look at it with weeping eyes, praying that the young man named Saul may yet be converted to God. "But," says one, "there are none of us who would be like Saul." No, you would not stone the saints, but perhaps those who do so would be permitted to lay their clothes at your feet. You do not invent the jest against the saints, but, perhaps, you repeat it and laugh at it and give countenance to those who use it.

There are many persons who are keepers of the clothes of open sinners. For instance, I believe that, very often, a merely moral man may exert a very detrimental influence upon sinners because they will say, "Look at So-and-so, he is not a Christian, yet he is a man of good repute." So they are led to believe that they may stay where he stays—out of Christ. O dear friends, may there be nothing about your walk and conversation that can be used to oppose the Gospel of Jesus Christ. There will be unless you are wholly on His side, for He Himself said, "He that is not with me is against me; and he that gathereth not with me scattereth abroad" (Matt. 12:30; Luke 11:23). If you are not on the side of Christ, you are on the side of His foes, for this is a fight that admits of no neutrality. If you cannot feel that you would, like Stephen, defend the cause of Christ, then, I fear, you only lack the opportunity and the circumstances, if not to stone Stephen, yet, at least, to let those who do the dreadful deed lay their clothes at your feet. The contrast recorded in our text is a very vivid one. I wish I could depict the equally vivid one between unconverted persons and Christians, for there is a contrast between them, a contrast that will come to this, one day, that there will be a great gulf fixed between them, across which there will be no passage. At the last great day, the righteous shall be upon the right hand of the Judge and the wicked upon His left hand. Christ Himself shall stand between them so that the division shall last as long as Christ Himself shall live.

A Remarkable Introduction of a Person to True Religion

Perhaps there may be someone here whom you know who has never yet come into contact with real, vital godliness, and you are very anxious that he should do so. I am equally anxious that he should. I think it ought to be your earnest endeavor that not only he, but all who are like him, should somehow or other come into contact with real religion. Now, as far as we see in the Bible, this is Saul's first introduction to anything like real Christianity. We have not his name before this verse in the Acts of the Apostles. So here, for the first time, he steps forward into the arena of conflict: a young man, whose name was Saul. Was he favorably impressed at once with Christ and His people? Certainly not, but quite the reverse. The impression made upon him was that of intense hatred and enmity toward Jesus of Nazareth and all His followers.

But, perhaps, he saw a bad specimen of Christianity; perhaps he listened to a very poor sermon that misrepresented the Gospel; perhaps he never saw any sign of the working of the Spirit. On the contrary, Saul's introduction to Christianity in the person of Stephen was of the most favorable kind. His own heart, however, was so desperately prejudiced against Christ that we find him no sooner brought into contact with Christianity than he becomes the keeper of the clothes of those who stoned the servant of the Lord.

Notice, then, what his introduction was. *He saw a Christian of the noblest type*—a man full of faith and of the Holy Spirit. He saw him at his best, for his face shone like the face of an angel. I wish that, when men of the world look upon us, they could see such Christians with shining faces. Perhaps, dear friend, the person about whom you are concerned may have taken a prejudice against true religion through the faults of believers. But that was not the case with Saul. I suppose that all the Christians that he had ever met with in Jerusalem—for it was the golden age of Christianity—were of the very best type as Stephen was. Yet, though he looked into that face which was burning with the light of grace and glory, he hated that face and gnashed his teeth against the man whose glorious, calm demeanor ought at once to have won him.

And then *he listened to a noble discourse*. It was a discourse specially fitted to the Jews. They always liked to hear the history of their nation. Their national pride was gratified by it. In after days, when Paul had to address them, he gave them a summary of their history very similar to this of Stephen, and wisely so. It was the best and most suitable discourse that could be given, yet the only result produced upon Saul and others was that they ran upon the preacher to stone him and put him to death. Now, dear friends, if you have brought some relative or friend to listen to the minister here, and the sermon seems to you to be most suitable and admirable, do not be surprised if, instead of seeing any good result come from it, you find, on the contrary, the provocation of the whole nature of the casual hearer and a stirring up of rebellion in his heart. Think it no new thing and no strange trial, for this was the case with the young man named Saul when he was introduced to a Christian with a shining countenance and to a ministry that was in all points admirable. Yet, for all that, he was the more hardened in his enmity against the Gospel of Jesus Christ.

But the young man named Saul saw something else. *He saw a Christian die a triumphant death.* How many have been converted by such a spectacle as that! There have been some who could ridicule the life and ministry of a Christian, but the dying speech—the bright and lustrous glance of the closing eye—the triumphant hymn of the departing saint—these have been irresistible arguments, and they have been compelled to yield to them. But it was not so with Saul, for we read after Stephen was put to death of "Saul, yet breathing out threatenings and slaughter against the disciples of the Lord" (Acts 9:1). Even that spectacle, which might have convinced an infidel, convinced not this young man whose name was Saul. And our first introduction of the Gospel to our friends may not at first end as hopefully as we could have wished and expected, yet we ought not to be discouraged, for Saul did become a Christian after all. It was no proof that he never would be converted that, at first, he grew more hardened. It was no evidence that the Gospel would not conquer his heart that, at first, his heart shut all its gates against Jesus Christ. We have a proverb that reminds us that Rome was not built in a day. We cannot always expect the New Jerusalem to be built in men's hearts in a single hour. There are some who are struck down at once, as Saul was afterward, but there are others against whose strong fortress the battering ram of truth must come with all its might year after year. It is only when God strikes the effectual blow of grace that, at last, they yield, subdued by almighty love.

At any rate, whether they yield or not, your duty is clear. Bring them to Christ; bring them under the sound of the Gospel. Do all that you can for their salvation so that if they will perish, when the funeral knell startles your ear, you will be able to say to yourself, "Whether he is lost or saved, I am not responsible. I am clear of his blood, for I told him the way of salvation. I pleaded with him for God, and I pleaded with God for him. I persuaded him to go with me and listen to the preaching of the Word. If he has rejected it and trampled it under foot, I cannot help it, though I would have helped it if I could. I must leave his fate in the hands of God." I think this case of Saul is a very encouraging one to any of you who are seeking to win sinners to the Savior. Did a man swear at you when you spoke to him about his soul? Well, there is sometimes more hope of a man who has enough grit in him to denounce me than of one who seems to agree with all that I say. He says, "Yes, sir; yes, sir; very good, sir"; and then passes it all off. Perhaps it shows that there is a bigger soul in the man even when he becomes a persecutor than when he simply waves his hand and says, "Go thy way for this time; when I have a convenient season, I will call for thee" (Acts 24:25). A downright opposition may only prove that there is good soil where we may sow the good seed of the kingdom.

An Instance of the Security of the Apostolical Succession

Do not be frightened at that expression. I am not a believer in that apostolical succession that is supposed to come by the laying of human hands upon human heads. But I believe that there has always been in the church of God a succession of faithful men so that when one has died, another has been called to take his place. I believe that it will always be so until Christ Himself shall come. *What a dreadful thing it was for the church to lose Stephen!* She had many useful men in her ranks, but Stephen seemed just then to come to the front. He had made a stir all over Jerusalem. Though specially appointed to look after the poor, there never was a deacon who was more thoroughly in the front rank of the church. He was worthy—I was going to say—to be an apostle for his holiness and daring. He convinced many of the truth of the Gospel of Christ. If he had been ill, his brethren and sisters would have prayed that his life might be preserved. If they had known that he was going to be put to death, they would have said, "It is better that we should die than that Stephen should. We cannot afford to lose him." It is a calamity for the church of Christ when her best men, whether ministers or deacons, are called home. Yet, dear friends, it often is the case that God takes His servants home just when they are most useful. When would you have Him take them home? When they are least useful? When they are little or no good here, you would let the Lord have them. That is not very generous on your part. The Lord is entitled to the very best. Some are getting ripe for glory, so it is but natural that the Master should take the ripest of them. You need not be astonished, therefore, when the most useful people are taken to heaven.

But now, look, Stephen is going home. Who will take Stephen's place? Do you not see him? The witnesses have laid their clothes at his feet, and no doubt Stephen's mantle was among them. So as surely as Elijah left his mantle to Elisha, *the mantle of Stephen was lying at the feet of Saul.* He did not put it on at once, but he did put it on afterward. And oftentimes, when men ask, "What shall we do when Mr. So-and-so has gone?" the Lord sends a man who does just as well as Mr. So-and-so has done. I have often been asked, "What is to be done with the Tabernacle and the College and the Orphanage when you are gone?" Dear me, the Lord got on very well before I was born, and I am sure He will when I am dead. That question never troubles me. Did you ever sit down and think, "What will my wife do when I am gone?" You do not like to think of it, then do not think of it, for it is no business of yours. The successor of any man whom God makes useful will be found in due course. He may be at present among the haters of the Gospel. He may be among those who are railing at the cross of Christ. Where was the great successor of John Huss found? Why, he is over there in a

German monastery. What! a monk? Yes, a monk, who goes crawling up
the stairs of the Santa Scala at Rome trying to get merit enough to save
his father and mother and himself and wishing he could always be there
accumulating merit! Yes, Martin Luther was the man to follow Huss,
and God raised him up in due time.

The saints in Jerusalem did not know where Stephen's successor
was, but God saw him among Stephen's enemies. He brought him out,
and Saul was a mightier apostle than Stephen could ever have been.
The church lost Stephen, but she gained Saul and that was a very good
exchange. Though nothing may be said that would be derogatory to
such a high-souled man as Stephen was, yet the church of Christ has
never had a servant who, taking him for all in all, has been so useful to
her as the famous apostle Paul, who was once that young man named
Saul. How much we owe, through divine grace, to his epistles for their
clear teaching of spiritual doctrines! No other apostle, though each one
was excellent in his own way, ever had so clear a revelation of or so
clearly taught those grand doctrines of grace that are the very backbone
of the Gospel of Jesus. And who else ever labored as he did? He says
himself—and he was always modest—"I laboured more abundantly
than they all: yet not I, but the grace of God which was with me" (1
Cor. 15:10). When Stephen was taken away, it was a great mercy that
he was succeeded by one who even surpassed him. And, my dear
friends, at this very time we need not be asking, "What shall we do
without So-and-so?" God has enough servants somewhere or other, and
we need not say, "Would that He would raise up more evangelists!" He
has already spied a man out in Chicago. Without going so far as that, he
could find one in any part of London or in any hamlet or village in the
country, wherever He chose to look for him. The Lord is never short of
men to serve Him. "Remember that Omnipotence has servants everywhere." And out of the ranks of Satan's army He can take the boldest
champion of evil, arrest him by almighty grace, and lay upon him the
charge to become a leader to the hosts of the living God. Never despair
and never doubt nor let even a desponding thought concerning Christ's
cause flit across your mind. They tell us that dark days are coming.
That is quite true, but the Sun of Righteousness will never be eclipsed.
They tell us that the powers of evil will grow stronger and stronger.
Suppose they do; the Almighty will never grow weak. We will fall back
upon the omnipotence and all sufficiency of Jehovah. Then we shall
know what it is not to feel any distrust or fear concerning the present or
the future of the church of the living God.

So, you see, in this case of Stephen and Saul, we have a clear instance of the certainty of true apostolical succession.

A Gracious Memorial of Repented Sin

Saul became Paul, and there is a great deal of good recorded of him under the name of Paul. But the Holy Spirit has caused this fact to be remembered, "The witnesses laid down their clothes at a young man's feet, whose name was Saul." Then does God write down the sins of His people before they are converted? Yes, He does. In this case, He writes it down in the Book of books so that, wherever the Bible goes, there goes the information that Saul of Tarsus was once a persecutor. When we read of Rahab, we are told that she was "the harlot." Why is this memorial kept of Saul's sins before conversion? *It was meant to keep Paul humble*, and it always did that. You notice how very sorrowfully he always speaks about this matter. He says that he was not meet to be called an apostle because he persecuted the church of God. Once, in speaking to the Lord, he said, "And when the blood of thy martyr Stephen was shed, I also was standing by, and consenting unto his death, and kept the raiment of them that slew him" (Acts 22:20). He never forgot that, and it always made him walk humbly before God. He wrote to Timothy, "I was before a blasphemer, and a persecutor, and injurious: but I obtained mercy" (1 Tim. 1:13).

Do not try, beloved, to forget your old sins. Let them ever be before you to keep you humble. I have heard of a certain high ecclesiastic who had been a fisherman. While he was rising in the world, he used to hang up his net that he might be reminded that he had once been a fisherman. At last, the pope made him a cardinal, and no one ever saw his net after that. They said that he had caught what he had fished for, so he put his net away. You and I had better always keep our nets in sight to remind us of what we once were. Look at the pit from whence you were digged, and when God gives you any special mercy, say to yourself, "What a miracle of grace is this, for I was among the most undeserving of all."

This sin of Paul's was always in his mind and so *it continually increased his love*. He was like the woman who loved much because she had had much forgiven. He was like the debtor who, although he owed the most, was most grateful because his lord had freely forgiven him all. Who was so zealous as Paul? He counted all things but loss for the glory of God. Surely that was because he felt himself to be a debtor beyond all others to the grace that had washed away the scarlet sin of murder from his guilty soul.

And, again, dear friends, this sin of Paul was recorded in the Bible, and retained in his memory because *it kept him to the doctrines of grace*. I have generally noticed that those professors who were always so very good and had nothing very marked about their conversion have gone off to that form of doctrine which I do not find in the Scriptures. But those of us who know how base we were before our conversion feel that there is only one kind of doctrine in which we can believe, and that is the doctrine of sovereign grace. It would take a great deal to grind me down into a belief in free will because it is contrary to my whole experience. I know this, if the Lord had not first loved me, I never would have loved Him. If there is any good thing in me whatsoever, it must have been implanted there by the Holy Spirit. If salvation be of works, then I can never have it. If it be the reward of natural goodness, then I shall never have it. I feel that it must be of grace and of grace alone. No doubt, the recollection of his sin helped to make Paul what he was—the grand evangelical preacher—the man who brought out the glorious doctrine of God's electing love—the man who, beyond all others, proclaimed the doctrine that salvation is of grace and grace alone and that God will have mercy on whom He will have mercy and will have compassion on whom He will have compassion. It would have been incompatible with the experience of the apostle to preach anything else. Therefore was the remembrance of his sin kept before him that he might always make known those precious truths.

And, perhaps, dear brethren and sisters, *this sin of Paul is recorded that he might always be hopeful about other people.* You know, from the moment he was converted to the moment he died, he was always a persecuted man. His life was divided into two periods: first he was persecutor, and then he was persecuted. When he had been driven from city to city and many times stoned, how he must have thought of Stephen and the stones that fell on him. When he had been hated of all men for Christ's sake, he might well have despaired of the Gospel ever spreading had he not said, "Ah! but, as it converted me, it can convert others. Did not I take care of the clothes of those who stoned Stephen— those rebels who took the pearls that fell from his lips and, like swine, trod them under foot?" This would encourage him to stand before the cruel Nero and to tell him the Gospel of Jesus, for He who could convert a Saul could convert a Nero if He willed to do it. You never find Paul drawing back or flinching, but he went preaching almost to the ends of the earth, feeling himself to be a debtor both to Jew and Gentile, barbarian, Scythian, bond and free, because, said he, "I obtained mercy, that in me first Jesus Christ might shew forth all longsuffering, for a pattern to them which should hereafter believe on him to life everlasting" (1 Tim. 1:16). Oh, yes! it is good for you to remember what you used to be, for you will have hope for other people when you remember that.

An Instance of the Overruling of God

If you look very carefully at it and look long enough, it will appear not altogether a bad thing that Saul should be there taking care of the clothes of the murderers of Stephen. Possibly you cannot, at first, see how any good can come out of it. But there never was a bad thing out of which God could not bring good. Even the death of Christ, which was the culmination of human sin, was the crowning point of divine love. *If Saul had not been there, Stephen would not have prayed for him.* But, Augustine says, in a sentence that is always quoted in every commentary on the Acts that I have seen, "If Stephen had not prayed, Paul had never preached." But Stephen's prayer, "Lord, lay not this sin to their charge," was such a comprehensive plea for his murderers that I can well conceive of his fixing his tearful gaze upon that young man named Saul and in his thoughts including him in that petition and beseeching the Lord not to lay it to his charge. And the Lord did not lay it to his charge, "because," says Paul, "I did it ignorantly in unbelief" (1 Tim. 1:13).

I believe it was a good thing for Saul to be there. I have sometimes thought when I have heard a man swear in the street, "That is an awful thing, but if he had not done' it, I would probably not have prayed for him." I always make it a rule to pray for a man when I hear him swear, so in that way God may bring good out of evil. Take care, all of you who love the Lord, whenever you hear or see anybody doing that which is wrong, always to pray, for this is the way we are to be the salt of the earth. The salt is always to be put where the putridity begins. This is the way in which we are to be the light of the world. The candles are to be brought when the darkness comes on. You do not need them until the sun has gone and the darkness has come. So, when you perceive the darkness, light your candles; when you perceive the putrefaction, scatter the salt by bringing the sinner before God in prayer.

But there is also something more than this. *If Saul had not been there, he would have missed the benefit of Stephen's discourse.* Stephen's sermon is the text from which Paul preached all his life. If you examine it carefully, you will find that Stephen's speech is the root out of which, through the blessing of the Spirit of God, Paul's theology grows. Stephen gives him the clue of all that argument in the epistle to the Romans about Sarah and Hagar, and all that discussion about Father Abraham being justified by faith is there in Stephen's speech. And the Epistle to the Hebrews is another plant that grows out of the seed that Stephen sowed in Saul's mind. There are several phrases that are identical. I think that the reason why we have that speech of Stephen recorded so fully is that Paul traveled with Luke, who wrote the Acts of the Apostles. Paul told Luke what Stephen had said, for it seems to have gone right into his soul and to have stuck there. It must have been so, for it molded all his epistles, and you can trace the influence of Stephen in every parchment upon which Paul put his pen. It may sometimes happen that men who are opposed to the Word of God may actually be influenced by a man at whom they sneered. That may be the very man at whose feet they humble themselves. Perhaps, after he is dead and gone, that man's piety may color the whole life of a young man who now hates him. You cannot tell. But this I know—out of many an evil thing, God has often brought great good, as He did in this case, both through the prayer and through the preaching of holy Stephen.

Whenever you think that an unconverted man has formed some plot to allure you into sin, have so much of the Holy Spirit about you that instead of his overcoming you, you will overcome him. Have you never heard of the soldier who reported that he had taken a prisoner? The officer said, "Bring him along, then." He said, "I cannot." "Why not?" "Because he is dragging me the other way," replied the soldier. He had not taken a prisoner; he had become a prisoner himself. Many a Christian man, instead of doing good to the world, is being led away captive by the world. Let it not be so with you. Make them turn to you, but do not you turn to them. It is well, in the firmness of faith, to draw them toward the Savior. But may it never happen that their evil example shall master your good and their revelry shall overcome your piety. God fill us with the Holy Spirit and with faith so that we may, like Stephen, be the means of transforming Saul, the persecutor, into Paul, the apostle.

I leave this subject with you, only asking you to pray for any whom you see to be distinguished for sin or infidelity or heresy. Pray God to save them. The more mischief they are doing, the more earnestly you ought to pray for them, for it is very likely that, if they were converted, the more good would they do. I read a strange speech of John Bunyan's once with which I did not wholly agree, though there was some truth in it. He said that he had great hope for the next generation because the young men that he met with were so intensely wicked, and he thought that if God, by His grace, changed them, they would make grand saints. So, when you meet with intensely wicked men, pray God to make grand saints of them. They are the raw material, ready to His hands, for Him to work upon. The very obstinacy and rebellion of their natures shows that when divine grace comes into them, they will make the most outspoken Christians. Therefore, pray for such. May God hear your prayer, for Jesus Christ's sake! Amen.

10

Paul's Sermon before Felix

And as he reasoned of righteousness, temperance, and judgment to come, Felix trembled, and answered, Go thy way for this time; when I have a convenient season, I will call for thee (Acts 24:25).

The power of the Gospel appears in marvelous grandeur when we see its hold upon hearts devoted to it, when subjected to trouble, persecution, and sorrow. How mighty must that Gospel be which, when it gained an entrance into the heart of Paul, could never be driven out of it! For it he suffered the loss of all things, and as for them, he counted them but dung that he might win Christ. To spread the truth, he encountered hardships, shipwrecks, perils on the land, and perils by sea. But none of these things moved him, neither did he count his life dear to him, that he might win Christ and be found in Him. Persecution followed persecution. By the Jews was he beaten with rods; he was dragged from one tribunal to another. Scarce in any city did he find anything but bonds and imprisonment awaiting him. Attacked in his own country, he is accused at Jerusalem and arraigned at Cesarea. He is taken from one tribunal to another to be tried for his life.

But mark how he always maintains the prominent passion of his soul. Put him where you may, he seems to be like John Bunyan who says, "If you let me out of prison today, I will preach the Gospel again tomorrow by the grace of God." No, more than that, he preached it in prison and before his judges he proclaimed it. Standing up before the Sanhedrim, he cries, "Touching the resurrection of the dead I am called in question" (Acts 24:21). When brought to stand before Agrippa, he tells out his conversion and so sweetly speaks of the grace of God that the king himself cries, "Almost thou persuadest me to be a Christian" (26:28). Here in our text, when he stands before the Roman procurator

---

This sermon was taken from *The Metropolitan Tabernacle Pulpit* and was preached on Sunday morning, January 10, 1858.

to be tried for life or death, instead of entering into a defense of himself, he reasons "of righteousness, temperance, and judgment to come," until his judge trembles. He that sits upon the throne takes the prisoner's place, while the prisoner judges him in anticipation of that time when the saints shall judge the angels as assessors with Christ Jesus.

Why, once let a man believe the Gospel and determine to spread it, and it makes him a grand man. If he be a man destitute of power, intellect, and talent, it makes him grandly earnest in his arduous desire to serve Christ in the little measure in which he can do it. But if he be a gifted man, it sets his whole soul on fire, brings out all his powers, develops everything that lies hidden, digs up every talent that had been buried in its napkin, and spreads out all the gold and silver of man's intellectual wealth, displaying it all to the honor of that Christ who has bought it all with His blood.

We might stay a little while and dilate on this thought and show you how in all ages this has been the truth, that the power of the Gospel has eminently moved in its influence over men's hearts, this proving the truth of that utterance of Paul when he said that neither tribulation, distress, persecution, famine, nakedness, peril, or sword shall separate them from the love of God that is in Jesus Christ their Lord. But instead of so doing, I invite you to contemplate the text more closely. We have before us a picture containing three characters: Felix and Drusilla, sitting side by side upon the judgment seat; Paul, the prisoner, brought in bound in chains to explain to Drusilla and Felix the doctrines of the Christian religion in order that he might either be acquitted or condemned to die. You have a judge extremely willing to put the prisoner to death because he desired to please the Jews. You have, on the other hand, a prisoner unabashed who comes before the judge and, without any debate, begins to unfold the Gospel, selecting a certain part of it described in our text as reasoning concerning "righteousness, temperance, and judgment to come." The judge trembles, dismisses the prisoner in haste, and promises to attend to him at a convenient season.

Note, first, then, *the appropriate sermon.* Note, secondly, *the affected audience*—for the audience was certainly moved—"Felix trembled"! Note, then, thirdly, *the lamentable disappointment.* Instead of attending to the message, "Go thy way" was all that Paul had.

The Appropriate Sermon

Just hear for a moment or two the history of Felix. Felix was originally a slave. He was freed by Claudius and became one of the infamous favorites of the emperor. Of course in that capacity he pandered to his master's vices and was at all times prepared to indulge the emperor in every lustful wish of his abominable heart. Through this he became promoted and ran through the stages of Roman preferment until he obtained the governorship of Judea. While he was governor there, he committed every act of extortion that it was possible for him to commit. He even went so far at last that the emperor Nero was obliged to recall him. He would have been severely punished for his crimes had it not been for the influence of his brother Pallas, another freed man with the emperor, through whom he obtained a release after a sharp rebuke. The Roman historian Tacitus says, "He exercised, in Judea, the imperial functions with a mercenary soul." You may easily see, then, how appropriate was the discourse when the apostle Paul reasoned concerning righteousness. Felix had been an unjust extortioner, and the apostle purposely selected righteousness to be a topic of his discourse.

By the side of Felix sat Drusilla. In the verse preceding our text she is called his wife. It is said she was a Jewess. This Drusilla was a daughter of Herod Agrippa, the great—a woman noted in that age for her superlative charms and unbridled voluptuousness. She had been once affianced to Antiochus, who, upon the death of Herod, refused to marry her. She was afterward married to Azizus, the king of the Amesenes, who, although a heathen, was so fond of her that he submitted to the most rigorous rites of the Jewish religion in order to obtain her in marriage. His love was but ill -requited, for in a little time she deserted him at the instigation of Felix and was, at the time of Paul's address, living as the wife of the lascivious Felix. We may easily understand then why the apostle Paul, fixing his stern eye on Drusilla, reasoned concerning continence and publicly rebuked both Felix and Drusilla for the shameless lust in which they were publicly living. And then you may imagine since there was now a court sitting and Felix himself was the judge and Paul the prisoner, how strikingly appropriate was the last theme—judgment to come.

I think it would not be very hard for us to imagine how well the apostle handled this subject. I can conceive that Felix expected to have a grand disquisition upon some recondite themes of the Gospel. Possibly he expected that the apostle Paul would reason concerning the resurrection of the dead. He thought perhaps that predestination, election, and free will would be the topics of the apostle's discourse. "Surely," thought he, "he will tell me those deep and hidden matters in which the Gospel of Jesus differs from Judaism." Not so. In another place on Mars' Hill, the apostle would speak of resurrection. In another place, he could speak of election and declare that God was the potter and man was but the clay. This was not the place for that nor the time for such subjects. This was the time for preaching the plain precepts of the Gospel and for dealing sternly with a wicked man who sat in eminent power. Conceive then the pointed manner of his opening discourse—how he would address Felix concerning righteousness. I can imagine how he would bring before the mind of Felix the widow who had been defrauded of inheritance, the fatherless children who, cast from affluence, were led to beg their bread. I can suppose how he brought before the mind of that base man the many bribes that he had taken when he sat upon his judgment seat. He would recall to him the false decisions that he had given. He would remind him how the Jews as a nation had been oppressed and how by taxation they had been ground to the earth. He would bring before him one scene after another where avarice had overridden equity, boldly and sternly depicting the exact character of the man, then at the end declaring that such men could have no inheritance in the kingdom of God and bidding him repent of this his wickedness that his sins might be forgiven him.

Then gently and delicately turning to the other subject, I can imagine how he would fix his eyes upon Drusilla and remind her that she had lost everything for which a woman ought to live, and he would solemnly bring the most powerful motives to bear upon her lascivious heart. Then turning to Felix, he would remind him that adulterers, fornicators, and unclean persons have no inheritance in the kingdom of God, reminding him how the vices of a ruler would tend to pollute a nation and how the iniquities of the nation of the Jews must in a great measure be laid to his charge. I can conceive how, for a moment, Felix would bite his lips. Paul gave him no time for anger and passion, for in a moment, in a fury of impassioned eloquence he introduced the judgment to come. He made Felix think he saw the Great White Throne, the books opened, and he himself arraigned before his judge. He made him hear the voices of the trumpet, the "Come ye blessed," the "Depart ye cursed." He petrified him, nailed him to his seat, opened his ears and made him listen while with stern and impassioned earnestness, though his hands were bound with chains, he used the liberty of the Gospel in upbraiding him. Well do I conceive that then Felix began to tremble. He that had been base and mean and perfidious trembled like a coward slave, as he really was. Though sitting on a throne, he pictured himself already damned. What he next would have done we cannot tell if the Devil had not then suggested to him that it was time to rise, for in hot haste he and Drusilla left the throne. "Go thy way for this time; when I have a convenient season, I will call for thee."

Hear me, then, brethren and sisters! What the apostle Paul did, every minister ought to do. He selected a topic appropriate to his audience. It is ours ever to do the same. But are there not to be found many ministers who, if they addressed kings and princes, would pour out before them the vilest adulation and flattery that ever came from mortal lips? Are there not many who, when they are aware that great and mighty ones are listening to them, trim their doctrine, cut the edges of their speech, and endeavor in some way or other to make themselves pleasing to their audience? Can there not be found many ministers who, if addressing an antinomian audience, would confine themselves strictly to predestination and reprobation? and ministers who, if they addressed an audience of philosophers, would just talk about morality but never mention such words as the covenant of grace and salvation by blood? Are there not some to be found who think the highest object of the minister is to attract the multitude and then to please them? O my God! How solemnly ought each of us to bewail our sin if we feel that we have been guilty in this matter. What is it to have pleased men? Is there anything in it that can make our heads lie easy on the pillow of our death? Is there anything in it that can give us boldness in the day of judgment or cause us happiness when we face Your tribunal, O Judge of quick and dead? No, my friends, we must always take our texts so that we may bear upon our hearers with all our might. I hope I may never preach *before* a congregation—I desire always to preach *to* you, nor do I wish to exhibit powers of eloquence, nor would I even pretend to exhibit any depth of learning. I would simply say, Hear me, my fellow men, for God does send me to you. There are some things that concern you; I will tell you of them. You are dying; many of you when you die must perish forever. It is not for me to be amusing you with some deep things that may instruct your intellect but do not enter your hearts. It is for me to fit the arrow to the string and send it home, to unsheathe the sword—be the scabbard never so glittering, to cast it aside—and let the majesty of naked truth smite at your hearts. For in the day of judgment, anything besides personal, homely speaking will be consumed as wood, hay, and stubble, but these shall abide, like the gold and silver and precious stones that cannot be consumed.

But some men will say, "Sir, ministers ought not to be personal." Ministers ought to be personal, and they will never be true to their Master until they are. I admire John Knox for going, Bible in hand, to Queen Mary and sternly upbraiding her. I admit I do not exactly love the way in which he did it, but the thing itself I love. The woman had been a sinner, and he told her so flat to her face. But now we poor craven sons of nobodies have to stand and talk about generalities. We are afraid to point you out and tell you of your sins personally. But, blessed be God, from that fear I have been delivered long ago. There walks not a man on the surface of this earth whom I dare not reprove. There are none of you, however connected with me by ties of profession or in any other respect, that I would blush to speak personally to as to the things of the kingdom of God. It is only by being bold, courageous, and sending home the truth that we shall at last be free from the blood of our hearers. May God grant us the power of Paul, that we may reason on appropriate subjects and not select generalities when we ought to be pushing home truths to the consciences of our hearers. After all, the apostle Paul needs no eulogy. The best eulogy that could be passed on the apostle was the fact that Felix trembled. And that brings us to the second part of our subject.

The Affected Audience

Yes, the poor prisoner, having nothing wherewith to assist him in the delivery of the truth but having everything to his disadvantage—the chain, the prison dress, the character of one that had stirred up sedition in a nation—this poor prisoner with believing hand laid hold on the sword of truth and with this he did divide assunder the joints and marrow. He did beard the lion in his den. Even now I see him look the governor sternly in the face, attack him in his heart, drive him from his excuses, push the word home at the point of the bayonet of truth, drive him from every refuge of lies, and make him tremble! O marvelous power of a preached Gospel! O mighty truth that God is with the ministry when the kings of the earth that take counsel together are yet dismayed by it. Who is he that does not see here something more than human eloquence, when a prisoner becomes the judge and the prince upon the throne becomes the criminal?

"Felix trembled." Have I not some here who have experienced the same feelings as Felix? Some plain spoken minister has told you something that was rather too plain for you. At first you were angry; on second thoughts, and as the man moved on in his discourse, you became chagrined that you had given him the opportunity of thus exposing you as you imagined. A better thought struck you, and you saw at once that the man could have no intention personally to insult you. Then your feelings changed. Thunderbolt after thunderbolt fell from his lips. He seemed a very Jupiter Tonans sitting upon his throne, casting lightnings from his lips. You began to tremble. "Verily here is a man that has told me all things that ever I did; is not this man sent from Christ?" Ah! and thus you have borne your witness to the truth of the Gospel. Though you have not felt its power to your salvation, yet you have been an unwilling witness that the Gospel has been true, for you have felt its power when it has made your knees knock together and your eyes run down with tears.

But what is it that makes men tremble under the sound of the Gospel? Some say it is their conscience. Yes, and doubtless it is in some sense. The poet said, "Conscience doth make cowards of us all" (Shakespeare, *Hamlet*). Certainly, when the minister's exposition is faithful and pertinent to our own case, conscience, if it be not thoroughly seared and dead, will make the blush mantle on our cheeks. But

I take it that conscience of itself is so thoroughly corrupt, together with all the other powers of manhood, that it would never even make a man go so far as trembling if there were not something at work upon the conscience besides its being left to its own natural force. My friends, I believe that what some people call natural conviction is, after all, the work of the Spirit. Some very profound divines are so fond of the doctrine that the Holy Spirit always works efficaciously that they think that the Spirit never can work a transitory emotion in a man's soul. They impute such things to conscience. And if they see a man like Felix trembling, they say 'tis all natural conscience! Now, do they not see that they are in this touching on another doctrine equally dear to them—the doctrine of total depravity? For if men be totally depraved by nature, then, as trembling is a good thing, they are not capable even of that without some influence of the Holy Spirit.

The fact is, my hearer, the Holy Spirit works in two ways. In some men's hearts He works with restraining grace only. The restraining grace, though it will not save them, is enough to keep them from breaking out into the open and corrupt vices in which some men indulge who are totally left by the restraints of the Spirit. Now, there was in Felix some little portion of this restraining grace. When the apostle laid the Gospel open to him, this restraining grace quickened the conscience and compelled Felix to tremble. Mark you, this grace man may resist and does resist.

For albeit the Holy Spirit is omnipotent and never can be resisted when He works omnipotently, yet as a strong man may sometimes not put out all his strength but work with his finger, for instance, so that he may permit even a gnat or an ant to overcome him, even so the Holy Spirit sometimes works but temporarily and but for good and excellent purposes, which He always accomplishes. But He allows men to quench and resist His influences so that salvation is not so much as approached thereby. God the Holy Spirit may work in men some good desires and feelings and yet have no design of saving them. But mark, none of these feelings are things that accompany sure salvation, for if so, they would be continued. But He does not work omnipotently to save except in the persons of His own elect, whom He assuredly brings to Himself. I believe, then, that the trembling of Felix is to be accounted for by the restraining grace of the Spirit quickening his conscience and making him tremble.

But what shall be said of some of you who never tremble? You have come here this morning with your brazen faces, and with your impudent and arrogant hearts. You have been mouthing high heaven with your blasphemies. Now you stand all unmoved and unabashed in the house of God. Though a Baxter should rise from the dead and with moving sighs and tears should preach the Gospel, you would laugh and scoff. Though Boanerges with a tongue of thunder should come and preach to you, you would turn up your lip and find some fault with his oratory, and his words would never reach your hearts. O ungodly generation! how has God given you up, and how has hell bewitched you? O race of evil doers! children that are corrupters! how are you seared. My soul reads with prophetic glance the handwriting on the wall! You are condemned already. You are past hope—"trees . . . twice dead, plucked up by the roots" (Jude 12). For in the fact that you tremble not there is proof not only of your death but of your positive corruption. You shall die as you are, without hope, without trust or refuge, for he that has lost feeling has lost hope. He that is past conscience God the Holy Spirit has given up, and He will no more strive with him forever.

The Lamentable Disappointment

Paul experienced disappointment when he saw Felix rise in haste and dismiss him from his presence. "It is wonderful," said a good man once to a minister, "it is wonderful to see a whole congregation moved to tears by the preaching of the Word." "Yes," said that minister, "it is wonderful. But I know a wonder ten times greater than that. The wonder is that those people should so soon wipe away their tears and forget what they have heard." 'Tis wonderful that Felix trembled before Paul; 'tis more wonderful that Felix should say, "Go your way." 'Tis strange, 'tis passing strange, that when the word touches the conscience, even then sin has such power over men that the truth can be repulsed and driven out of the heart. Felix, unhappy Felix! why is it that you rise from your judgment seat? Is it that you have much business to do? Stop, Felix; let Paul speak to you a minute longer. You have business. But have you no business for your soul? Stop, unhappy man! Are you about again to be extortionate, again to make your personal riches greater? Oh, stop! Can you not spare another minute for your poor soul? It is to live forever. Have you nothing laid up for it—no hope in heaven, no blood of Christ, no pardon of sin, no sanctifying Spirit, no imputed righteousness? Ah! man, there will be a time when the business that seems so important to you will prove to have been but a daydream, a poor substitute for the solid realities you have forgotten. Do you reply, "No, the king has sent me an urgent commission. I must attend to Caesar." Ah! Felix, but you have a greater monarch than Caesar. There is one who is Emperor of heaven and Lord of earth. Can you spare no time to attend to His commands? Before His presence Caesar is but a worm. Man, will you obey the one and despise the other? Ah! no; I know what you dare not say. Felix, you are turning aside again to indulge in your lascivious pleasures. Go, and Drusilla with you!

But stop! Dare you do that with that last word ringing in your ears—judgment to come. What! will you repeat that wanton dalliance that has damned you already, and will you go again to imbrue your hands in lust and doubly damn your spirit after warnings heard and felt? O man! I could weep over you, to think that as the bullock goes to the slaughter and as the lamb licks the knife, so you go back to the sin that destroys you and to the lust that ruins you. You, too, many of you, have often been impressed under the ministry. I know what you have said on the Monday morning, after deep searchings of heart on Sunday. You have said, "I must attend to business. I must see after the things of this world." Ah! you will say that one day when hell shall laugh you in the face for your folly. Think of men that are dying every day saying, "We must live" and forgetting that they must die! O poor soul! to be caring about that house, your body, and neglecting the tenant within! Another replies, "I must have a little more pleasure." Pleasure do you call it? What! can there be pleasure in turning suicide to your own soul—pleasure in defying your Maker, trampling on His laws, despising His grace? If this be pleasure, 'tis a pleasure over which angels might weep. What, man, will you count this pleasure when you come to die? Above all, will you count this pleasure when you stand before your Maker's bar at last? It is a strange delusion that causes you to believe a lie. There is no pleasure in that which brings wrath upon your soul, even to the uttermost.

But the usual reply is, "There is time enough yet." The young man says, "Let me alone until I grow old." And you old men, what do you say? I can suppose that the youth looks forward to life and expects to find a future time more convenient. But there are some of you over whose heads seventy winters have blown. When do you hope to find a convenient season? You are within a few days' march of the tomb. If you do but open your poor dull eyes, you may see death but a slight distance in advance. The young *may* die; the old *must!* To sleep in youth is to sleep in a siege; to sleep in old age is to slumber during the attack. What! man, will you that are so near your Maker's bar still put Him off with a "Go thy way"? What! procrastinate now, when the knife is at your throat, when the worm is at the heart of the tree and the branches have begun to wither, when the grinders fail even now because they are few and they that look out of the windows are darkened? The sere and yellow leaf has come upon you, and you are still unready for your doom! O man! of all fools, a fool with a gray head is the worst fool anywhere. With one foot in the grave and another foot on a sandy foundation, how shall I depict you but by saying to you, as God said to the rich man, You fool! a few more nights and your soul shall be required of you. Then where are you?

But still the common cry is, "There is time enough." Even the worldly moralist said, "Time enough is always little enough." Time enough, man! What for? Surely you have spent time enough in sin. The time past may "suffice us to have wrought the will of the Gentiles" (1 Peter 4:3). What! time enough to serve a God that laid down His life for you? No! eternity will not be too long to utter His praise, and therefore it cannot be too long to love Him here and serve Him the few remaining days that you are to live on earth. But stop! I will reason with you. Come, Felix, you shall not go away this morning until my whole soul has poured itself out over you, not until I have cast my arms around you and tried to stop you this time from turning from the face of Him that bids you live. You say, "Another time." How do you know that you will ever feel again as you feel now? This morning, perhaps, a voice is saying in your heart, "Prepare to meet your God." Tomorrow that voice will be hushed. The gaieties of the ballroom and the theater will put out that voice that warns you now, and perhaps you will never hear it again. Men all have their warnings, and all men who perish have had a last warning. Perhaps this is your last warning. You are told today that except you repent, you must perish; except you put your trust in Christ, you must be cast away forever. Perhaps no honest lip will again warn you. Perhaps no tearful eye will ever look on you affectionately again. God today is pulling the reins tight to check you from your lust. Perhaps, if today you spurn the bit and rush madly on, He will throw the reins upon your back saying, "Let him alone." Then it is a dark steeplechase between earth and hell, and you will run it in mad confusion, never thinking of a hell until you find yourself past warning, past repentance, past faith, past hope.

But again, how do you know if you should ever have these feelings again God will accept you then? "To day," He says. "To day, if ye will hear his voice, harden not your hearts" (Heb. 3:7–8). This hour His love weeps over you, and His bowels yearn for you. Today He says, "Come now, and let us reason together, . . . though your sins be as scarlet, they shall be as white as snow; though they be red like crimson, they shall be as wool" (Isa. 1:18). Do you today turn a deaf ear to Him? Do you today forego His invitation and despise His warning? Take heed! You may one day need what now you despise. You may then cry to Him, but He will not hear you. You may then pray to Him, but He will shut out your prayer. His only answer will be, "*I called!* Remember the Surrey Music Hall that morning! *I called, and you refused!* You stood against that pillar under the gallery. *I called and you refused! I stretched out My hands*, as if I would bring you to My bosom, and *no one regarded* Me. You were there in the gallery. You listened, but it was as though you heard not. Therefore"—and oh! the dreadful conclusion!—"*I also will*

laugh at your calamity. I will mock when your fear comes" (see Prov.
1:24, 26). Stay! Those are not my words. They are God's words. Turn
to the book of Proverbs and find them there. It were a harsh thing for
me to say of God. But God says it of Himself, and God is true, though
every man be a liar. If He be true, how do you know that He may not
despise your prayer one day, shut out your cry, and banish you forever?

But again, how do you know that you shall live to be warned again?
Said a minister once, when I gently hinted to him that he had not
preached the Gospel that morning, "No, I did not mean to preach to sinners in the morning. But I will preach to them in the evening." "Ah!"
said I, "but what if some of your congregation of the morning should be
in hell before the evening." So may I say to you. You have promised to
go to a friend's house today. You think you cannot break that promise.
You wish you could. You wish you could go home and fall on your
knees and pray. But no, you cannot, because your promise binds you.
You will have a convenient season one of these days! And so God
Almighty is to wait man's convenience. How do you know you will live
until that convenience comes? A little too much heat or too much cold
within the brain—a little too fast flowing of the blood or a little too
slow circulation thereof—some little turning of the fluids of the body in
a wrong direction, and you are dead!

> Dangers stand thick through all the ground,
>> To bear you to the tomb,
> And fierce diseases wait around,
>> To hurry mortals home.

Oh! why will you then dare to procrastinate and say, "Time enough
yet"? Will your soul ever be saved by your saying, "Time enough yet"?
Archbishop Tillotson well says, "A man might say I resolve to eat, but the
resolve to eat would never feed his body. A man might say, I am resolved
to drink, but the resolve to drink would never shake his thirst." And you
may say, "I am resolved, by and by, to seek God." But your resolve will
not save you. It is not the forgetful hearer, but the doer, of the Word that
shall be blessed therein. Oh, that you might now say: Today, my God,
today I confess my sin. Today I ask you to manifest Your grace. Today receive my guilty soul and show me a Savior's blood. Today I renounce my
follies, my vices, and my sins, constrained by sovereign grace. Today I
cast away my good works as my ground of trust. Today I cry,

> Nothing in my hands I bring,
> Simply to Thy cross I cling.

Oh! happy minister who shall have such an audience! happier than
Paul, if he should know that his congregation had said this! Come, O

Holy Spirit, and draw unwilling hearts and make them bow before the scepter of sovereign grace.

Preaching, you see, takes away my voice. Ah! it is not that. It is not the preaching, but the sighing over your souls that is the hard work. I could preach forever. I could stand here day and night to tell my Master's love and warn poor souls. But 'tis the afterthought that will follow me when I descend these pulpit steps that many of you, my hearers, will neglect this warning. You will go; you will walk into the street. You will joke; you will laugh. My Master says, "Son of man, have you heard what the children of Israel say concerning you? Behold, you are as one that plays a tune upon an instrument; they make merry with you, and they go their ways" (see Ezek. 33:32). Yes, but that were little. To be laughed at is no great hardship to me. I can delight in scoffs and jeers. Caricatures, lampoons, and slanders are my glory. Of these things I boast, yes, in these I will rejoice. But that you should turn from your own mercy—this is my sorrow. Spit on me, but oh! repent! Laugh at me, but oh! believe in my Master! Make my body as the dirt of the streets, if you will, but damn not your own souls! Oh! do not despise your own mercies. Put not away from you the Gospel of Christ. There are many other ways of playing a fool besides that. Carry coals in your bosom; knock your head against a wall. But do not damn your souls for the mere sake of being a fool, for fools to laugh at. Oh! be in earnest upon an earnest subject. If there be no hereafter, live as you like. If there be no heaven, if there be no hell, laugh at me. But if these things be true and if you believe them, I charge you, as I shall face you at the judgment bar of the Lord Jesus in the day of judgment—I charge you, by your own immortal welfare, lay these things to heart. Prepare to meet your God, O son of Israel! And the Lord help you in this thing, for Jesus' sake. Amen.

11

Paul—His Cloak and His Books

The cloak that I left at Troas with Carpus, when thou comest, bring with thee, and the books, but especially the parchments (2 Timothy 4:13).

Foolish persons have made remarks upon the trifles of Scripture. They have marveled why so little a matter as a cloak should be mentioned in an inspired book. But they ought to know that this is one of the many indications that the book is by the same author as the book of nature. Are there not things that our shortsightedness would call trifles in the volume of creation around us? What is the peculiar value of the daisy upon the lawn or the buttercup in the meadow? Compared with the rolling sea or the eternal hills, how inconsiderable they seem! Why has the hummingbird a plumage so wondrously bejeweled, and why is so much marvelous skill expended upon the wing of a butterfly? why such curious machinery in the foot of a fly or such a matchless optical arrangement in the eye of a spider? Because to most men these are trifles, are they to be left out of nature's plans? no, because greatness of divine skill is as apparent in the minute as in the magnificent. Even so in Holy Writ, the little things that are embalmed in the amber of inspiration are far from inappropriate or unwise.

Besides, in providence are there not trifles? It is not every day that a nation is rent by revolution or a throne shaken by rebellion. Far more often a bird's nest is destroyed by a child or an anthill overturned by a spade. It is not at every hour that a torrent inundates a province, but how frequently do the dewdrops moisten the green leaves? We do not often read of hurricanes, tornadoes, and earthquakes, but the annals of

---

This sermon was taken from *The Metropolitan Tabernacle Pulpit* and was preached on Sunday morning, November 29, 1863.

providence could reveal the history of many a grain of dust borne along in the summer's gale, many a sere leaf rent from the poplar, and many a rush waving by the river's brim. Hence learn to see, in the littles of the Bible, the God of providence and nature. Observe two pictures, and you will, if thoroughly skilled in art, detect certain minute details that indicate the same authorship if they are by the same hand. The very littlenesses often, to men of artistic eye, will betray the painter more certainly than the more prominent strokes that might far more easily be counterfeited. Experts detect a handwriting by a slight quivering in the upstrokes, the turn of the final mark, a dot, a cross, or less matters still. Can we not see the legible handwriting of the God of nature and providence in the very fact that the sublimities of revelation are interspersed with homely, everyday remarks? But they are not trifles, after all. I venture to say that my text has much in it of spiritual instruction. I trust that *this cloak* may warm your hearts this morning, that *these books* may give you instruction, and that *the apostle* himself may be to you an example of heroism, fitted to stir your minds to imitation.

This Cloak

Troas was a principal seaport town of Asia Minor. Very likely the apostle Paul was seized at Troas on the second occasion of his being taken before the Roman emperor. The soldiers usually appropriated to themselves any extra garment in the possession of an arrested person, such things being considered as the perquisites of those who made the arrest. The apostle may have been forewarned of his seizure and therefore prudently committed his few books and his outer garment, which made up all his household stuff, to the care of a certain honest man named Carpus. Although Troas was a full six hundred miles' journey from Rome, yet the apostle Paul is too poor to purchase a garment and so directs Timothy, as he is coming that way, to bring his cloak. He needs it much, for the sharp winter is coming on, and the dungeon is very, very chilly. This is a brief detail of the circumstances. What kind of cloak it was, certain learned commentators have spent whole pages in trying to discover. But as we know nothing at all about it ourselves, we will leave the question to them, believing that they know as much as we do but no more.

But what does the cloak teach us? There are five or six lessons in it.

The first is this—let us perceive here with admiration, *the complete self-sacrifice of the apostle Paul for the Lord's sake.* Remember, my dear friends, what the apostle once was. He was great, famous, and wealthy. He had been brought up at the feet of Gamaliel. He was so zealous among his brethren that he could not but have commanded their sincere respect. He was attended by a guard of soldiers when he went from Jerusalem to Damascus. I do not know whether the horse on which he rode was his own, but he must have been a man of importance to have been allotted so important a post in religious matters. He was a man of good standing in society, and doubtless, everybody looking at young Saul of Tarsus would have said, "He will make a great man. He has every chance in life. He has a liberal education, a zealous temperament, abundant gifts, and the general esteem of the Jewish rulers. He will rise to eminence." But when the Lord met him that day on the road to Damascus, how everything changed with him! Then he could truly say, "But what things were gain to me, those I counted loss for Christ. Yea doubtless, and I count all things but loss for the excellency of the knowledge of Christ Jesus my Lord: for whom I have suffered the loss of all things, and do count them but dung, that I may win Christ, and be found in him" (Phil. 3:7–9).

He begins to preach—away goes his character. Now, nothing is too bad for Paul among his Jewish associates. "Away with such a fellow from the earth: for it is not fit that he should live" (Acts 22:22) was the exact expression of Jewish feeling toward him. He continues his labors and away has gone his wealth. He has either scattered it among the poor or it has been sequestered by his former friends. He journeys from place to place at no small sacrifice of comfort. The wife to whom he was probably once united—for no unmarried man could vote in Sanhedrim as Paul did against Stephen—had fallen sick and died, and the apostle now preferred a life of singleness that he might give himself entirely to his work. If in this world only he had hope, he would have been of all men the most miserable. He has at length grown gray, and now the very men who owed their conversion to him have forsaken him. When he first came into Rome they stood with him, but now they have all gone like winter's leaves. The poor old man, "such an one as Paul the aged" (Philem. 9), sits with nothing in all the world to call property but an old cloak and a few books, and those are six hundred miles away. Ah! how he emptied himself and to what extremity of destitution was he willing to bring himself for Christ's sake. Do not complain that he mentions his clothes. A greater than he did so and did so in an hour more solemn than that in which Paul wrote the epistle. Remember who it was that said, "They parted my garments among them, and upon my vesture did they cast lots" (John 19:24). The Savior must die in absolute nakedness, and the apostle is made something like him as he sits shivering in the cold.

Friends, was Paul right in all this? Were his sacrifices reasonable? Was the object that he contemplated worthy of all this suffering and self-denial? Was he carried away by an excessive heat of fanaticism to spend upon an inferior object what was not required of him? No

believer here thinks so. You all believe that if you could give up substance, talent, and esteem, yes, and your own life also for Christ, it
would be well spent. I say you think so, but how many of us have ever
carried it out? Had I not better say, how few of us? There are some who
seldom have an opportunity for sacrificing for Christ at all. What they
give is spared from their superfluity; they never feel it. It is a high lux-
ury when a man has such a love for Jesus that he is able to give until he
pinches himself. If Paul were reasonable, what are you and I? If Paul
only gives as a Christian should do, how ashamed should we be of ourselves? If he will bring himself to poverty for Christ, what shall we say
of those base-born professors who will not lose a trifle in their trade for
honesty's sake? What shall we say of those who say, "I know how to
get money, and I know how to keep it too," and look with scorn upon
those who are more generous than they. If you are content to condemn
Paul and charge him with folly, do so. But if not, if this be but a reasonable service and such as the infinite grace of God which Paul experienced required of him, then let us do something of the like sort. If you
have experienced as much love, love the Lord as much, and spend and
be spent for the Lord Jesus.

Secondly, dear friends, we learn *how utterly forsaken the apostle
was by his friends.* If he had not a cloak of his own, could not some of
them lend him one? Ten years before, the apostle was brought in chains
along the Appian Way to Rome. Fifty miles before he reached Rome, a
little band of members of the church came to meet him. When he came
within twenty miles of the city, at the Three Taverns, there came a still
larger posse of the disciples to escort him so that the chained prisoner
Paul went into Rome attended by all the believers in that city. He was
then a younger man, but now for some reason or other, ten years afterward, nobody comes to visit him. He is confined in prison, and they do
not even know where he is so that Onesiphorus, when he comes to
Rome, has to seek him out very diligently. He is as obscure as if he had
never had a name. Though he is still as great and glorious an apostle as
ever, men have so forgotten him and the church has so despised him
that he is friendless. The Philippian church, ten years before, had made
a collection for him when he was in prison. Though he had learned in
whatsoever state he was to be content, yet he thanked them for their
contribution as an offering of a sweet-smelling savor to God. Now he is
old, and no church remembers him. He is brought to trial, and there are
Eubulus and Pudens and Linus—will not some of them stand by his
side when he is brought before the emperor? "At my first answer no
man stood with me" (2 Tim. 4:16). Poor soul, he served his God and
worked himself down to poverty for the church's sake, yet the church
has forsaken him! Oh! how great must have been the anguish of the

loving heart of Paul at such ingratitude. Why did not the few who were in Rome, if they had been never so poor, make a contribution for him? Could not those who were of Caesar's household have found a cloak for the apostle? No; he is so utterly left that although he is ready to die of ague in the dungeon, not a soul will lend or give him a cloak.

What patience does this teach to those similarly situated! Has it fallen to your lot, my brother or sister, to be forsaken of friends? Were there other times when your name was the symbol of popularity, when many lived in your favor like insects in your sunbeam. And has it come to this now, that you are forgotten as a dead man out of mind? In your greatest trials do you find your fewest friends? Have those who once loved and respected you fallen asleep in Jesus? And have others turned out to be hypocritical and untrue? What are you to do now? You are to remember this case of the apostle. It is put here for your comfort. He had to pass through as deep waters as any that you are called to ford, and yet remember, he says, "Notwithstanding the Lord stood with me, and strengthened me." So now, when man deserts you, God will be your friend. This God is our God forever and ever—not in sunshiny weather only, but forever and ever. This God is our God in dark nights as well as in bright days. Go to Him, spread your complaint before Him. Murmur not. If Paul had to suffer desertion, you must not expect better usage. Let not your faith fail you as though some new thing had happened to you. This is common to the saints. David had his Ahithophel, Christ His Judas, Paul his Demas, and can you expect to fare better than they? As you look at that old cloak, as it speaks of human ingratitude, be of good courage and wait on the Lord, for He shall strengthen your heart. "Wait, I say, on the LORD" (Ps. 27:14).

There is a third lesson. Our text shows *the apostle's independence of mind*. Why did not the apostle borrow a cloak? Why did not he beg one? No, no, no. That is not to the apostle's taste at all. He has a cloak, and though it is six hundred miles away, he will wait until it comes. Though there may be some that may lend, he knows that they who go a borrowing go a sorrowing and that they who beg are seldom welcome. I do not think a Christian man should blush to borrow or to beg if he be absolutely brought to it, but I never like that class of people who do either systematically. I wish many of the poor would not damage the charity of others by being so ready to beg on every pretense of necessity. A Christian man would do well to remember that it is never to his honor, though it is not always to his dishonor, to beg. "I cannot dig; to beg I am ashamed" (Luke 16:3), said the unfaithful steward, and if he had been a faithful one, he would have been more ashamed still. I say again, when it comes to the pinch and a man must ask of his fellow, let him do it boldly. But let him never be too ready to do it, but, like the apostle, as long as he can do without it, let him say, I have labored with my own hand and have eaten no man's bread for nothing (see 2 Thess. 3:8). He taught that the minister of God had a right to be supported by the people. If you partake of their spirituals, says he, it is right that you give of your temporals. He insists upon it that they are not to muzzle the mouth of the ox that treads out the corn. Yet, though he holds this as a great general principle, he never takes anything himself. He follows his trade of tent making. He stitches away at the canvas and earns his own living so that he is chargeable to no man. Noble example! How anxious all Christians ought to have been to see that he did not come to want in his old age! Yet he does come to poverty. But his independent spirit is not broken to the last, for he will wait until his own cloak is brought six hundred miles rather than ask any man to give or to lend. Let the Christian man be quite as independent, for though independence is not a Christian grace, yet it is a common grace that when wreathed with Christianity is very beautiful and benefits the character of a son of God.

The fourth remark is: see here, *how very little the apostles thought about how they were dressed.* Paul wants enough to keep him warm. He asks no more. There is no doubt whatever that the other parts of his garments were getting very dilapidated—that he was indeed in a state of rags and so he needed the cloak to wrap about him. We read in olden times of many of the most eminent servants of God being dressed in the poorest manner. When good Bishop Hooper was led out to be burned, he had been long in prison. His clothes were so gone from him that he borrowed an old scholar's gown, full of rags and holes, that he might put it on and went limping with pains of sciatica and rheumatism to the stake. We read of Jerome of Prague that he lay in a damp, cold dungeon and was refused anything to cover him in his nakedness and cold. Some ministers are very careful lest they should not always be dressed in a canonical or gentlemanly manner. I like that remark of Whitefield's when someone of a bad character wondered how he could preach without out a cassock. "Ah," he said, "I can preach without a cassock, but I cannot preach without a character." What matters the outward garment so long as the character be right?

This is a lesson to our private members too. We sometimes hear them say, "I could not come out on the Sabbath. I had no fit clothes to come in." Any clothes are fit to come to the house of God with if they are paid for, no matter how coarse they may be. If they are the best God has given you, do not murmur. Inasmuch as the trial of raiment is a very sharp one to some of the poorest of God's people, I think this text was put into the Bible for their comfort. Your Master wore no soft and dainty raiment. His garment was the simple peasant's smock frock, woven from the top throughout without seam, and yet He never blushed to wear it in the presence of kings and priests. I shall always believe that the Christian ought to cultivate a noble indifference to these outward things. But when it comes to the pinch of absolute want of clothing, then he may comfort himself in this thought, "Now am I companion with the Master. Now do I walk in the same temptation as the apostles. Now I suffer even as they also suffered." Every saint is an image of Christ, but a poor saint is His express image, for Christ was poor. So, if you are brought to such a pitch with regard to poverty that you scarcely know how to provide things decent by way of raiment, do not be dispirited but say, "My Master suffered the same, and so did the apostle Paul." So take heart, and be of good cheer.

Paul's cloak at Troas shows me *how mighty the apostle was to resist temptation.* "I do not see that," you say. The apostle had the gift of miracles. Our Savior, though able to work miracles, never wrought anything like a miracle on His own account nor did His apostles. Miraculous gifts were entrusted to them with Gospel ends and purposes, for the good of others and for the promotion of the truth but never for themselves. Our Savior was tempted of the Devil, you will remember, when He was hungry, to turn stones into bread. That was a strong temptation to apply miraculous powers that were intended for other ends to His own comfort. But He rebuked Satan and said, "Man shall not live by bread alone" (Matt. 4:4). Paul also had power to have created a cloak if he had liked. Why could he not? His very shadow healed the sick. If he had willed it, he could have prevented the cold and damp from having any effect upon himself. He who had once raised to life dead Eutychus, when he had fallen from a loft, and brought back the vital heat could certainly have kept the heat in his own body if he had chosen. And I am bold to say the Devil often came to him and said, "If you be an apostle of God, if you can work miracles, command this atmosphere to rise in temperature or these rags to be joined together to form a comfortable raiment." You do not know—you cannot tell, for you were never put to it—what were the stern struggles the apostle must have had in resisting the foul temptation to use his miraculous gifts for himself.

O friends, I am afraid you and I are much more ready to give way to self than was the apostle. We preach the Gospel, and if God helps us, oh! directly the Devil will have us to take some of the praise. "You preached a good sermon this morning," said one to John Bunyan as he came down the stairs. "You are too late," said honest John, "the Devil told me that when I was preaching." Yes, we work the miracles but take the honor of it to ourselves. There is the temptation to any man who has gifts to use them to his own purposes. If he does, he is an unfaithful steward to his Master. I do beseech you, whether in the Sunday school or the church, never let the miracle-working power that God has given you be used for yourselves. You can do for Christ's sake mighty things through faith and prayer, but never let prayer and faith be prostituted to so base a purpose as to minister to the flesh. I know carnal minds will not comprehend this, but spiritual minds who know the temptations of the Devil will know how stern must be a lifelong battle to keep ourselves back from doing that which might apparently make us happy but which would at the same time make us unholy.

The sixth lesson from this cloak is we are taught in this passage *how precisely similar one child of God is to another*. I know we look upon Abraham, Isaac, and Jacob as being very great and blessed beings—we think that they lived in a higher region than we do. We cannot think that if they had lived in these times they would have been Abraham, Isaac, and Jacob. We suppose that these are very bad days and that any great height of grace or self-denial is not very easily attainable. My own conviction is that if Abraham, Isaac, and Jacob had lived now, instead of being less, they would have been greater saints—for they only lived in the dawn, and we live in the noon. We hear the apostles often called *Saint* Peter and *Saint* Paul. Thus they are set up on high as on an elevated niche. If we had seen Peter and Paul, we should have thought them very ordinary sort of people—wonderfully like ourselves. If we had gone into their daily lives and trials, we should have said, "Well, you are wonderfully superior to what I am in grace. But somehow or other, you are men of like passions with me. I have a quick temper; so have you, Peter. I have a thorn in the flesh; so have you, Paul. I have a sick house; Peter's wife's mother lies sick of a fever. I complain of the rheumatism, and the apostle Paul, when aged, feels the cold and wants his cloak."

Ah, we must not consider the Bible as a book intended for transcendental superelevated souls—it is an everyday book. These good people were everyday people, only they had more grace, but we can get more grace as well as they could. The fountain at which they drew is quite as full and as free to us as to them. We have only to believe after their fashion and trust to Jesus after their way, and although our trials are the same as theirs, we shall overcome through the blood of the Lamb. I do like to see religion brought out in everyday life. Do not tell me about the godliness of the Tabernacle, tell me about the godliness of your shop, your counter, and your kitchen. Let me see how grace enables you to be patient in the cold or joyful in hunger or industrious in labor. Though grace is no common thing, yet it shines best in common things. To preach a sermon or to sing a hymn is but a paltry thing compared with the power to suffer cold and hunger and nakedness for Christ's sake. Courage then, courage then, fellow pilgrim, the road was not smoothed for Paul any more than it is for us. There was no royal road to heaven in those days other than there is even now. They had to go through sloughs and bogs and mire as we do still.

> They wrestled hard as we do now
> With sins, and doubts, and fears.

But they have gained the victory at last, and even so shall we. So much then for the cloak that was left at Troas with Carpus.

These Books

Look at Paul's books. We do not know what the books were about, and we can only form some guess as to what the parchments were. Paul had a few books that were left, perhaps wrapped up in the cloak, and Timothy was to be careful to bring them. *Even an apostle must read.* Some of our very ultra-Calvinistic brethren think that a minister who reads books and studies his sermon must be a very deplorable specimen of a preacher. A man who comes up into the pulpit, professes to take his text on the spot, and talks any quantity of nonsense is the idol of many. If he will speak without premeditation, or pretend to do so, and never produce what they call a dish of dead men's brains—oh! that is the preacher. How rebuked are they by the apostle! He is inspired, and yet he wants books! He has been preaching at least for thirty years, and yet he wants books! He had seen the Lord, and yet he wants books! He had had a wider experience than most men, and yet he wants books! He had been caught up into the third heaven and had heard things that it was unlawful for a man to utter, yet he wants books! He had written the major part of the New Testament, and yet he wants books! The apostle says to Timothy and so he says to every preacher, "Give attendance to reading" (1 Tim. 4:13). The man who never reads will never be read; he who never quotes will never be quoted. He who will not use the thoughts of other men's brains proves that he has no brains of his own. Friends, what is true of ministers is true of all our people. You need to read. Renounce as much as you will all light litera-ture, but study as much as possible sound theological works, especially the Puritanic writers and expositions of the Bible. We are quite per-suaded that the very best way for you to be spending your leisure is to be either reading or praying. You may get much instruction from books that afterward you may use as a true weapon in your Lord and Master's service. Paul cries, "Bring the books"—join in the cry.

Our second remark is that *the apostle is not ashamed to confess that he does read.* He is writing to his young son Timothy. Now, some old preachers never like to say a thing that will let the young ones into their secrets. They suppose they must put on a very dignified air and make a mystery of their sermonizing. But all this is alien from the spirit of truthfulness. Paul wants books and is not ashamed to tell Timothy that he does. Timothy may go and tell Tychicus and Titus if he likes—Paul does not care.

Paul herein is a picture of industry. He is in prison; he cannot preach. What will he do? As he cannot preach, he will read. As we read of the fishermen of old and their boats, the fishermen were gone out of them. What were they doing? Mending their nets. So if providence has laid you upon a sickbed and you cannot teach your class—if you cannot be working for God in public—mend your nets by reading. If one occupation is taken from you, take another, and let the books of the apostle read you a lesson of industry.

He says, "especially the parchments." I think the books were Latin and Greek works, but that the parchments were Oriental. Possibly they were the parchments of Holy Scripture. Or as likely, they were his own parchments, on which were written the originals of his letters that stand in our Bible as the epistles to the Ephesians, the Philippians, the Colossians, and so on. Now, it must be "especially the parchments" with all our reading; let it be *especially the Bible.* Do you attach no weight to this advice? This advice is more needed in England now than almost at any other time, for the number of persons who read the Bible, I believe, is becoming smaller every day. Persons read the views of their denominations as set forth in the periodicals; they read the views of their leader as set forth in his sermons or his works, but the Book, the good old Book, the divine fountainhead from which all revelation wells up—this is too often left. You may go to human puddles until you forsake the clear crystal stream that flows from the throne of God. Read the books, by all manner of means, but especially the parchments. Search human literature, if you will, but especially stand fast by that Book which is infallible, the revelation of our Lord and Savior Jesus Christ.

The Apostle

It is almost too dark to see him—we will find him out in that frightful den! The horrid dungeon—the filth lies upon the floor until it looks like a road that is seldom scraped—the draught blows through the only little slit, which they call a window. The poor old man, without his cloak, wraps his ragged garment about him. Sometimes you see him kneeling down to pray, and then he dips his pen into the ink and writes to his dear son Timothy. No companion, except Luke, who occasionally comes in for a short time. Now, how shall we find the old man? What sort of temper will he be in?

We find him *full of confidence in the religion that has cost him so much.* For in the first chapter, at the twelfth verse, we hear him say, "For the which cause I also suffer these things: nevertheless I am not ashamed: for I know whom I have believed, and am persuaded that he is able to keep that which I have committed unto him against that day." No doubt, often the Tempter said to him, "Paul, why you have lost everything for your religion! It has brought you to beggary. See, you have preached it, and what is the reward of it? The very men you have converted have forsaken you. Give it up, give it up, it cannot be worth all this. Why, they will not even bring you a cloak to wrap around you. You are left here to shiver, and very soon your head will be struck from your body. Take off your hand from the standard and retire." "No," says the apostle, "I *know* whom I have believed." Why, I have heard of professors who say, "Ever since I have been a Christian I have lost in my business, and therefore I will give it up." But our beloved apostle clings to it with a life grip. And oh, there is no heart in our piety if our afflictions make us doubt the truth of our religion, for these trials, inasmuch as they work patience and patience experience and experience hope, render us such that we are not ashamed, but we do the yet more firmly hold on to Christ. Just think you hear the apostle say, "I know whom I believe." It is very easy for *us* to say it. We are very comfortable, sitting easily in our pews. We shall go home to our plentiful meal. We shall be clothed comfortably. We have friends about us who will smile at us, and it is not hard to say, "I know whom I have believed." But if you were vexed on the one hand by Hermogenes and Philetus and on the other hand by Alexander the coppersmith and Demas, you would not find it quite so easy to say, "The Lord is faithful" (2 Thess. 3:3). Behold this noble champion who is just as much unmoved at the worst as he was at the best times. I know how to be full, said he once. Now he can say, I know how to suffer hunger. I know how to abound and how to suffer loss (see Phil. 4:12).

But he is not only confident. You will notice that this grand old man is *having communion with Jesus Christ in his sufferings.* Turn to the second chapter, at the tenth verse. Did ever sweeter language than this come from anyone? "Therefore I endure all things for the elect's sakes, that they may also obtain the salvation which is in Christ Jesus with eternal glory. It is a faithful saying: For if we be dead with him, we shall also live with him: if we suffer, we shall also reign with him; if we deny him, he also will deny us: if we believe not, yet he abideth faithful: he cannot deny himself." Ah, there are two in the dungeon—not only the man who is suffering trouble as an evildoer, even to bonds, but there sits with him one like to the Son of Man, sharing all his griefs and bearing all his despondencies and so lifting up his head. Well may the apostle rejoice that he has fellowship with Christ in His sufferings, being made conformable to His death.

Nor is this all. Not only is he confident for the past and in sweet communion for the present, but *he is resigned for the future*. Look at the fourth chapter and the sixth verse. "I am now ready to be offered, and the time of my departure is at hand." It is a beautiful emblem taken from the sacrificial bullock. There it is, tied to the horns of the altar and ready to be offered. So the apostle stands as a sacrifice ready to be offered upon the altar. I am afraid that we cannot all say we are ready to be offered. Paul was ready to be a burnt offering. If God willed it, he would be burned to ashes at the stake. Or he would be a drink offering, as he did become when a stream of blood flowed under the sharp sword. He was ready to be a peace offering, if God willed it, to die in his bed. In any case, he was a free-will offering to God. For he offered himself voluntarily, as he says, "I am now ready to be offered, and the time of my departure is at hand." Glorious old man! Many a professed Christian has been clothed in scarlet and fared sumptuously every day and yet never could say he was ready to be offered but looked upon the time of his departure with grief and sorrow. As you think, then, of poor, shivering, ragged Paul, think of the jewel that he carried in his breast. O you sons of poverty, recollect that the magnificence of a holy life and the grandeur and nobility of a consecrated heart can deliver you altogether from any shame that may cling to your rags and poverty. For as the sun at setting paints the clouds with all the colors of heaven, so your very rags and poverty and shame may make your life the more illustrious as the splendor of your piety lights them with heavenly radiance.

We have not quite concluded with the apostle, for we find him not only resigned but *triumphant*. "I have fought a good fight, I have finished my course, I have kept the faith" (2 Tim. 4:7). See the Grecian warrior just returned from battle. He has many wounds, and there is a gash across his brow. His breast is streaming here and there with cuts and flesh wounds. One arm is dislocated. He halts, like Jacob, on his thigh. He is covered with the smoke and dust of battle. He is besmeared with many a blood splash. He is faint and weary and ready to die, but what does he say? As he lifts up his right arm with his buckler tightly clasped upon it, he cries, "I have fought a good fight, I have kept my shield." That was the object of ambition with every Grecian warrior. If he kept his shield he came home glorious. Now, faith is the Christian's shield. And here I see the apostle, though he wears all the marks of the conflict, yet he triumphs in these marks of the Lord Jesus, saying, "I have fought a good fight. My very scars and wounds prove it. I have kept the faith." He looks to that golden buckler of the faith fastened to his arm and rejoices in it. The tyrant Nero never had such triumph as the apostle Paul, nor did all the warriors of Rome when the multitudes climbed the chimney tops and looked down upon the procession. None of them had such true glory as this solitary man who has trodden the winepress alone, who has stood against the lion, a solitary champion, with no eye to pity and no arm to save, still triumphant to the end. Brave spirit! never mind the old cloak at Troas, so long as your faith is safe.

He not only triumphs in the present, but *he is in expectation of a crown.* When the Grecian wrestler had fought a good fight, a crown was presented to him. So Paul, who writes about the old cloak, also writes, "Henceforth there is laid up for me a crown of righteousness, which the Lord, the righteous judge, shall give me at that day: and not to me only, but unto all them also that love his appearing" (v. 8). When I was picturing Paul and talking of the poverty of many believers—"Ah," said the sinner, "Who would be a Christian? Who would suffer so much for Christ? Who would lose everything as Paul did?" Worldly minds here are thinking, "What a fool, to be led away by such an excitement!" Ah! but see how the tables have turned! "Henceforth there is laid up for me a crown"! What if he had been robed in scarlet, had rolled in wealth, and had been great, but there had been no crown for him in heaven, no joy hereafter, and a fearful looking for of judgment? See, he springs from his dungeon to his throne. Nero may cut off his head, but that head shall wear a starry crown. Courage, then, you that are downtrodden, afflicted, and despairing, be of good cheer, for the end will make up for the way, and all the roughness of the pilgrimage will be well recompensed by the glory that awaits all those who are resting upon Christ Jesus.

We close, having done with this old cloak, when we say, is it not beautiful as you read this epistle, and, indeed all the apostle's letters, to see how *everything that the apostle thought of was connected with Christ,* how he had concentrated every passion, every power, every thought, every act, every word and set the whole upon Christ. I believe that there are many who love Christ after a sort, just as the sun shines today. But you know if you concentrate the rays of that sun with a burning glass and fix all the rays upon any object, then what heat there is, what burning, what flame, what fire! So many men scatter their love and admiration on almost every creature, and Christ gets a little, as we all get some rays of the sun. But he is the man who, like the apostle Paul, brings all his thoughts and words to a focus. Then he burns his way through life. His heart is on fire; like coals of juniper are his words. He is a man of force and energy. He may have no cloak, yet for all that he is a great man, and the czar in his imperial mantle is but a driveling dwarf by the side of this giant in the army of God.

O, I wish we could set our thoughts on Christ this morning. Are we trusting in Him this morning? Is He all our salvation and all our desire? If He be, then let us live to Him. Those who are wholly Christ's are not many. O that we were espoused as chaste virgins to Christ that we might have no other lover and know no other object of delight. Blind be these eyes to all but Christ; deaf be these ears to any music but the voice of Christ; lame be these feet to any way but that of obedience to Him; palsied be these hands to anything but work for Him; dead be this heart to every joy if Jesus cannot move. Even as a straw floats upon the river and is carried to the ocean, so would I be bereft of all power and will to do anything but that which my Lord would have me do, and be carried along by the stream of His grace right onward, ready to be offered up or ready to live, ready to suffer or ready to reign just as He wills, only that He may be served in my living and dying. It will little matter what cloak you wear or if you have not any at all if you have but such a concentration of all your bodily and mental powers and spiritual energies upon Christ Jesus and upon Him alone. May those of you who have never trusted Jesus be ready to rely upon Him now. He did not forsake Paul, even in extremity, and He will not forsake you.

> Trust him, he will ne'er deceive you,
> Though you hardly of him deem;
> He will never, never leave you,
> Nor will let you quite leave him.

Therefore trust him now and ever, for Jesus' sake. Amen.

12

The Story of
a Runaway Slave

Perhaps he therefore departed for a season, that thou shouldest receive him for ever (Philemon 15).

Nature is selfish, but grace is loving. He who boasts that he cares for nobody and nobody cares for him is the reverse of a Christian, for Jesus Christ enlarges the heart when He cleanses it. None is so tender and sympathetic as our Master, and if we be truly His disciples, the same mind will be in us that was also in Christ Jesus. The apostle Paul was eminently largehearted and sympathetic. Surely he had enough to do at Rome to bear his own troubles and to preach the Gospel. If, like the priest in the parable of the good Samaritan, he had passed by on the other side, he might have been excused, for he was on the urgent business of that Master who once said to His seventy messengers, "Salute no man by the way" (Luke 10:4). We might not have wondered if he had said, "I cannot find time to attend to the wants of a runaway slave." But Paul was not of that mind. He had been preaching, and Onesimus had been converted. Henceforth he regarded him as his own son.

I do not know why Onesimus came to Paul. Perhaps he went to him as a great many scapegraces have come to me—because their fathers knew me and so, as Onesimus's master had known Paul, the servant applied to his master's friend, perhaps to beg some little help in his extremity. Anyhow, Paul seized the opportunity and preached to him Jesus, and the runaway slave became a believer in the Lord Jesus Christ. Paul watched him, admired the character of his convert, and was glad to be served by him. When he thought it right that he should return

---

This sermon was taken from *The Metropolitan Tabernacle Pulpit* and was preached at the Metropolitan Tabernacle, Newington.

to his master, Philemon, he took a deal of trouble to compose a letter of apology for him—a letter that shows long thinking, since every word is well selected. Albeit the Holy Spirit dictated it, inspiration does not prevent a man's exercising thought and care on what he writes. Every word is chosen for a purpose. If he had been pleading for himself, he could not have pleaded more earnestly or wisely.

Paul, as you know, was not accustomed to write letters with his own hand but dictated to an amanuensis. It is supposed that he had an affliction of the eyes. Therefore when he did write he used large capital letters, as he says in one of the epistles, "Ye see how large a letter I have written unto you with my own hand" (Gal. 6:11). The epistle was not a large one, but he probably alluded to the largeness of the characters that he was obliged to use whenever he himself wrote. This letter to Philemon, at least part of it, was not dictated but was written by his own hand. See the nineteenth verse. "I Paul have written it with mine own hand, I will repay it." It is the only note of hand that I recollect in Scripture, but there it is—an IOU for whatever amount Onesimus may have stolen.

Let us cultivate a largehearted spirit and sympathize with the people of God, especially with new converts if we find them in trouble through past wrongdoing. If anything needs setting right, do not let us condemn them offhand and say, "You have been stealing from your master, have you? You profess to be converted, but we do not believe it." Such suspicious and severe treatment may be deserved, but it is not such as the love of Christ would suggest. Try and set the fallen ones right, and give them again, as we say, "a fair start in the world." If God has forgiven them, surely we may, and if Jesus Christ has received them, they cannot be too bad for us to receive. Let us do for them what Jesus would have done had He been here; so shall we truly be the disciples of Jesus.

Thus I introduce to you the text, and I notice concerning it, first that it contains *a singular instance of divine grace.* Secondly, it brings before us *a case of sin overruled.* And, thirdly, it may be regarded as *an example of relationship improved by grace,* for now he that was a servant for a season will abide with Philemon all his lifetime and be no more a servant but a brother beloved.

An Instance of Divine Grace

We see the grace of God in Onesimus's *election.* He was a slave. In those days slaves were very ignorant, untaught, and degraded. Being barbarously used, they were for the most part themselves sunk in the lowest barbarism, neither did their masters attempt to raise them out of it. It is possible that Philemon's attempt to do good to Onesimus may have been irksome to the man, and he may therefore have fled from his house. His master's prayers, warnings, and Christian regulations may have been disagreeable to him, and therefore he ran away. He wronged his master, which he could scarcely have done if he had not been treated as a confidential servant to some extent. Possibly the unusual kindness of Philemon and the trust reposed in him may have been too much for his untrained nature. We know not what he stole, but evidently he had taken something, for the apostle says, "If he hath wronged thee, or oweth thee ought, put that on mine account" (v. 18). He ran away from Colosse, therefore, and thinking that he would be less likely to be discovered by the ministers of justice, he sought the city of Rome, which was then as large as the city of London now is and perhaps larger. There in those back slums, such as the Jews' quarter in Rome now is, Onesimus would go and hide, or amongst those gangs of thieves that infested the imperial city; he would not be known or heard of any more, so he thought. He could live the free and easy life of a thief. Yet, mark you, the Lord looked out of heaven with an eye of love and set that eye on Onesimus.

Were there no free men that God must elect a slave? Were there no faithful servants that He must choose one who had embezzled his master's money? Were there none of the educated and polite that He must needs look upon a barbarian? Were there none among the moral and the excellent that infinite love should fix itself upon this degraded being who was now mixed up with the very scum of society? And what the scum of society was in old Rome I should not like to think, for the upper classes were about as brutalized in their general habits as we can very well conceive, and what the lowest scum of all must have been, none of us can tell. Onesimus was part and parcel of the dregs of a sink of sin. Read Paul's first chapter of the Epistle to the Romans, if you can, and you will see in what a horrible state the heathen world was at that time, and Onesimus was among the worst of the worst. Yet eternal love, which passed by kings and princes and left Pharisees and Sadducees, philosophers and magi, to stumble in the dark as they chose, fixed its eye upon this poor benighted creature that he might be made a vessel to honor, fit for the Master's use.

> When the Eternal bows the skies
> To visit earthly things,
> With scorn divine he turns his eyes
> From towers of haughty kings.
>
> He bids his awful chariot roll
> Far downward from the skies,
> To visit every humble soul,
> With pleasure in his eyes.

> Why should the Lord that reigns above
>   Disdain so lofty kings?
> Say, Lord, and why such looks of love
>   Upon such worthless things?
>
> Mortals, be dumb; what creature dares
>   Dispute his awful will?
> Ask no account of his affairs,
>   But tremble and be still.
>
> Just like his nature is his grace,
>   All sovereign, and àll free;
> Great God, how searchless are thy ways,
>   How deep thy judgments be!

"I will have mercy on whom I will have mercy, and I will have compassion on whom I will have compassion" (Rom. 9:15; see also Exod. 33:19) rolls like thunder alike from the cross of Calvary and from the mount of Sinai. The Lord is a sovereign and does as He pleases. Let us admire that marvelous, electing love that selected such a one as Onesimus!

Grace also is to be observed, in the next place, in the *conversion* of this runaway slave. Look at him! How unlikely he appears to become a convert. He is an Asiatic slave of about the same grade as an ordinary Lascar or heathen Chinese. He was, however, worse than the ordinary Lascar, who is certainly free and probably an honest man, if he is nothing else. This man had been dishonest, and he was daring withal, for after taking his master's property he was bold enough to make a long journey from Colosse to reach Rome. But everlasting love means to convert the man and converted he shall be. He may have heard Paul preach at Colosse and Athens, but he had not been impressed. At Rome, Paul was not preaching in St. Peter's. It was in no such noble building. Paul was not preaching in a place like the Tabernacle where Onesimus could have a comfortable seat—no such place as that. But it was probably down there at the back of the Palatine hill, where the Praetorian Guard have their lodgings and where there was a prison called the Praetorium. In a bare room in the barracks prison Paul sat, with a soldier chained to his hand, preaching to all who were admitted to hear him. There it was that the grace of God reached the heart of this wild young man. Oh, what a change it made in him immediately! Now you see him repenting of his sin, grieved to think he has wronged a good man, vexed to see the depravity of his heart as well as the error of his life. He weeps. Paul preaches to him Christ crucified, and the glance of joy is in his eyes and from that heavy heart a load is taken. New thoughts light up that dark mind. The very face is changed and the entire man renewed, for the grace of God can turn the lion to a lamb, the raven to a dove.

Some of us, I have no doubt, are quite as wonderful instances of divine election and effectual calling as Onesimus was. Let us, therefore, record the loving-kindness of the Lord, and let us say to ourselves, "Christ shall have the glory of it. The Lord has done it and to the Lord be honor, world without end."

The grace of God was conspicuous in *the character that it wrought in Onesimus* upon his conversion, for he appears to have been helpful, useful, and profitable. So Paul says. Paul was willing to have had him as an associate, and it is not every man that is converted that we should altogether choose as a companion. There are odd people to be met with who will go to heaven, we have no doubt, for they are pilgrims on the right way, but we would like to keep on the other side of the road. They are cross-grained, and there is a something about them that one's nature can no more delight in than the palate can take pleasure in nauseous physic. They are a sort of spiritual hedgehogs. They are alive and useful, and no doubt they illustrate the wisdom and patience of God, but they are not good companions. One would not like to carry one of them in his bosom. But Onesimus was evidently of a kind, tender, loving spirit. Paul at once called him brother and would have liked to retain him. When he sent him back, was it not a clear proof of change of heart in Onesimus that he would go back? Away as he was in Rome, he might have passed on from one town to another and have remained perfectly free, but, feeling that he was under some kind of bond to his master—especially since he had injured him—he takes Paul's advice to return to his old position. He will go back and take a letter of apology or introduction to his master. He feels that it is his duty to make reparation for the wrong that he has done.

I always like to see a resolve to make restitution of former wrongs in people who profess to be converted. If they have taken any money wrongfully, they ought to repay it. It were well if they returned sevenfold. If we have in any way robbed or wronged another, I think the first instincts of grace in the heart will suggest compensation in all ways within our power. Do not think it is to be gotten over by saying, "God has forgiven me, and therefore I may leave it." No, dear friend, but, inasmuch as God has forgiven you, try to undo all the wrong and prove the sincerity of your repentance by so doing. So Onesimus will go back to Philemon and work out his term of years with him or otherwise do Philemon's wishes. For though he might have preferred to wait upon Paul, his first duty was due to the man whom he had injured. That showed a gentle, humble, honest, upright spirit. Let Onesimus be commended for it. No, let the grace of God be extolled for it. Look at the difference between the man who robbed and the man who now comes back to be profitable to his master.

What wonders the grace of God has done! Friends, let me add: What wonders the grace of God can do! Many plans are employed in the world for the reformation of the wicked and the reclaiming of the fallen. To every one of these, as far as they are rightly bottomed, we wish good success, for whatever things are lovely and pure and of good report, we wish them God speed. But mark this word—the true reforming of the drunkard lies in giving him a new heart; the true reclaiming of the harlot is to be found in a renewed nature. Purity will never come to fallen women by those hideous Contagious Diseases Acts that, to my mind, wear, like Cain, a curse upon their foreheads. Womanhood will but sink the lower under such laws. The harlot must be washed in the Savior's blood, or she will never be clean. The lowest strata of society will never be brought into the light of virtue, sobriety, and purity except by Jesus Christ and His Gospel. We must stick to that. Let all others do what they like, but God forbid that I should glory save in the Cross of our Lord Jesus Christ. I see certain of my brethren fiddling away at the branches of the tree of vice with their wooden saws. But as for the Gospel, it lays the ax at the roots of the whole forest of evil. If it be fairly received into the heart, it fells all the upas trees at once, and instead of them there spring up the fir tree, the pine tree, and the box tree together to beautify the house of our Master's glory. Let us, when we see what the Spirit of God can do for men, publish the grace of God and extol it with all our might.

A Case of Sin Overruled

Onesimus had no right to rob his master and run away. But God was pleased to make use of that crime for his conversion. It brought him to Rome and so brought him where Paul was preaching. Thus it brought him to Christ and to his right mind. Now, when we speak of this, we must be cautious. When Paul says, "Perhaps he . . . departed for a season, that thou shouldest receive him for ever" (Philem. 15), he does not excuse his departure. He does not make it out that Onesimus did right—not for a moment. Sin is sin, and, whatever sin may be overruled to do, yet sin is still sin. The crucifixion of our Savior has brought the greatest conceivable blessings upon mankind, yet nonetheless it was with wicked hands that they took Jesus and crucified Him. The selling of Joseph into Egypt was the means in the hands of God of the preservation of Jacob and his sons in the time of famine. But his brethren had nothing to do with that, and they were nonetheless guilty for having sold their brother for a slave. Let it always be remembered that the faultiness or virtue of an act is not contingent upon the result of that act. If, for instance, a man who has been set on a railway to turn the switch forgets to do it, you call it a very great crime if the train comes to mischief and a dozen people are killed. Yes, but the crime is the same if nobody is killed. It is not the result of the carelessness but the carelessness itself that deserves punishment. If it were the man's duty to turn the switch in such-and-such a way, and his not doing so should even by some strange accident turn to the saving of life, the man would be equally blameworthy. There would be no credit due to him, for if his duty lies in a certain line his fault also lies in a certain line, namely, the neglecting of that duty. So if God overrules sin for good, as He sometimes does, it is nonetheless sin. It is sin just as much as ever, only there is so much the more glory to the wonderful wisdom and grace of God who out of evil brings forth good and so does what only omnipotent wisdom can perform. Onesimus is not excused, then, for having embezzled his master's goods nor for having left him without right. He still is a transgressor, but God's grace is glorified.

Remember, too, that this must be noticed—that when Onesimus left his master he was performing an action the results of which, in all probability, would have been ruinous to him. He was living as a trusted dependent beneath the roof of a kind master who had a church in his house. If I read the epistle rightly, he had a godly mistress and a godly master, and he had an opportunity of learning the Gospel continually. But this reckless young blade, very likely, could not bear it and could have lived more contentedly with a heathen master who would have beaten him one day and made him drunk another. The Christian master he could not bear, so away he went. He threw away the opportunities of salvation, and he went to Rome. He must have gone into the lowest part of the city and associated, as I have already told you, with the very grossest company. Now, had it come to pass that he had joined in the insurrections of the slaves that took place frequently about that time, as he in all probability would have done had not grace prevented, he would have been put to death as others had been. He would have had short shrift in Rome. Half suspect a man and off with his head was the rule toward slaves and vagabonds. Onesimus was just the very man that would have been likely to be hurried to death and to eternal destruction. He had put his head, as it were, between the lion's jaws by what he had done. When a young man suddenly leaves home and goes to London, we know what it means. When his friends do not know where he is, and he does not want them to know, we are aware, within a little, where he is and what he is at. What Onesimus was doing I do not know, but he was certainly doing his best to ruin himself. His course, therefore, is to be judged, as far as he is concerned, by what it was likely to bring him to and though it did not bring him to it, that was no credit to him, but all the honor of it is due to the overruling power of God.

See, dear brethren, how God overruled all. Thus had the Lord purposed. Nobody shall be able to touch the heart of Onesimus but Paul. Onesimus is living at Colosse; Paul cannot come there, he is in prison. It is needful, then, that Onesimus should be gotten to Paul. Suppose the kindness of Philemon's heart had prompted him to say to Onesimus, "I want you to go to Rome and find Paul out and hear him." This naughty servant would have said, "I am not going to risk my life to hear a sermon. If I go with the money you are sending to Paul or with the letter, I shall deliver it, but I want none of his preaching." Sometimes, you know, when people are brought to hear a preacher with the view of their being converted, if they have any idea of it, it is about the very last thing likely to happen because they go there resolved to be fireproof, and so the preaching does not come home to them. It would probably have been just so with Onesimus. No, no, he was not to be won in that way, he must be gotten to Rome another way.

How shall it be done? Well, the Devil shall do it, not knowing that he will be losing a willing servant thereby. The Devil tempts Onesimus to steal. Onesimus does it, and when he has stolen he is afraid of being discovered. So he makes tracks for Rome as quickly as he can and gets down among the back slums. There he feels what the prodigal felt—a hungry belly, and that is one of the best preachers in the world to some people. Their conscience is reached in that way. Being very hungry, not knowing what to do and no man giving anything to him, he thinks whether there is anybody in Rome that would take pity on him. He does not know anybody in Rome at all and is likely to starve. Perhaps one morning there was a Christian woman—I should not wonder—who was going to hear Paul. She saw this poor man sitting crouched up on the steps of a temple and went to him and spoke about his soul. "Soul," said he, "I care nothing about that, but my body would thank you for something to eat. I am starving." She replied, "Come with me, then," and she gave him bread. Then she said, "I do this for Jesus Christ's sake." "Jesus Christ!" he said, "I have heard of Him. I used to hear of Him over at Colosse." "Whom did you hear speak about Him?" the woman would ask. "Why, a short man with weak eyes, a great preacher named Paul who used to come to my master's house." "Why, I am going to hear him preach," the woman would say. "Will you come and hear him with me?" "Well, I think I should like to hear him again. He always had a kind word to say to the poor."

So he goes in and pushes his way among the soldiers. Paul's Master incites Paul to speak the right word. It may have been so, or it may have been the other way—that not knowing anybody else at all, he thought, "Well, there is Paul, I know. He is here a prisoner, and I will go down and see what prison he is in." He goes down to the Praetorium and finds him there, tells him of his extreme poverty, and Paul talks to him. Then he confesses the wrong he has done, and Paul, after teaching him a little while, says, "Now, you must go back and make amends to your master for the wrong you have done." It may have been either of these ways. At any rate, the Lord must have Onesimus in Rome to hear Paul, and the sin of Onesimus, though perfectly voluntary on his part so that God had no hand in it, is yet overruled by a mysterious providence to bring him where the Gospel shall be blessed to his soul.

Now, I want to speak to some of you Christian people about this matter. Have you a son who has left home? Is he a willful, wayward young man who has gone away because he could not bear the restraints of a Christian family? It is a sad thing it should be so—a very sad thing. But do not despond or even have a thought of despair about him. You do not know where he is, but God does. You cannot follow him, but the Spirit of God can. He is going a voyage to Shanghai. Ah, there may be a Paul at Shanghai who is to be the means of his salvation, and as that Paul is not in England, your son must go there. Is it to Australia that he is going? There may be a word spoken there by the blessing of God to your son that is the only word that ever will reach him. I cannot speak it. Nobody in London can speak it, but the man there will. God, therefore, is letting him go away in all his willfulness and folly that he may be brought under the means of grace that will prove effectual to his salvation.

Many a sailor boy has been wild, reckless, godless, Christless, and at last has gotten into a foreign hospital. Ah, if his mother knew that he was down with the yellow fever, how sad her mind would be, for she would conclude that her dear son will die away at Havana or somewhere and never come home again. But it is just in that hospital that God means to meet with him. A sailor writes to me something like that. He says, "My mother asked me to read a chapter every day, but I never did. I got into the hospital at Havannah, and when I lay there, there was a man near to me who was dying. He died one night, but before he died he said to me, 'Mate, could you come here? I want to speak to you. I have got something that is very precious to me here. I was a wild fellow, but reading this packet of sermons has brought me to the Savior. I am dying with a good hope through grace. Now, when I am dead and gone, will you take these sermons and read them? May God bless them to you. And will you write a letter to the man that preached and printed those sermons to tell him that God blessed them to my conversion? And that I hope He will bless them to you.'" It was a packet of my sermons, and how God did bless them to that young man who, I have no doubt whatever, went to that hospital because there a man who had been brought to Christ would hand to him the words that God had blessed to himself and would bless to his friend. You do not know, dear mother, you do not know. The worst thing that can happen to a young man is sometimes the best thing that can happen to him.

I have sometimes thought when I have seen young men of position and wealth taking to racing and all sorts of dissipation, Well, it is a dreadfully bad thing, but they may as well get through their money as quickly as ever they can. Then when they have gotten down to beggary they will be like the young gentleman in the parable who left his father." When he had spent all, there arose a mighty famine in that land, and he began to be in want. He said, "I will arise and go to my father." Perhaps the disease that follows vice—perhaps the poverty that comes like an armed man after extravagance and debauch—is but love in another form sent to compel the sinner to come to himself and consider his ways and seek an ever merciful God.

You Christian people often see the little gutter children—the poor little arabs in the street—and you feel much pity for them, as well you may. There is a dear sister here, Miss Annie Macpherson, who lives only for them. God bless her and her work! When you see them you cannot be glad to see them as they are, but I have often thought that the poverty and hunger of one of these poor little children has a louder voice to most hearts than their vice and ignorance. God knew that we were not ready and able to hear the cry of the child's sin, and so He added the child's hunger to that cry, that it might pierce our hearts. People could live in sin and yet be happy if they were well-to-do and rich. If sin did not make parents poor and wretched and their children miserable, we should not see it. Therefore we should not arouse ourselves to grapple with it. It is a blessing, you know, in some diseases when the patient can throw the complaint out upon the skin. It is a horrible thing to see it on the skin, but still it is better than its being hidden inside. Oftentimes the outward sin and the outward misery are a sort of throwing out of the disease so that the eyes of those who know where the healing medicine is to be had are thereby drawn to the disease, and so the soul's secret malady is dealt with.

Onesimus might have stopped at home and might never have been a thief, but he might have been lost through self-righteousness. Now his sin is visible. The scapegrace has displayed the depravity of his heart, and now it is that he comes under Paul's eye and Paul's prayer and becomes converted. Do not, I pray you, ever despair of men or women or children because you see their sin upon the surface of their characters. On the contrary, say to yourself, "This is placed where I can see it that I may pray about it. It is thrown out under my eye that I may now concern myself to bring this poor soul to Jesus Christ, the mighty Savior, who can save the most forlorn sinner." Look at it in the light of earnest, active benevolence, and arouse yourselves to conquer it. Our duty is to hope on and to pray on. It may be, perhaps, that "he therefore departed for a season, that thou shouldest receive him forever." Perhaps the boy has been so wayward that his sin may come to a crisis and a new heart may be given him. Perhaps your daughter's evil has been developed that now the Lord may convince her of sin and bring her to the Savior's feet. At any rate, if the case be ever so bad, hope in God and pray on.

An Example of Relations Improved

"He therefore departed for a season, that thou shouldest receive him forever; not now as a servant, but . . . a brother beloved, specially to me, but how much more unto thee?" You know we are a long while learning great truths. Perhaps Philemon had not quite found out that it was wrong for him to have a slave. Some men who were very good in their time did not know it. John Newton did not know that he was doing wrong in the slave trade. George Whitefield, when he left slaves, which had been willed to him, to the orphanage at Savannah, did not think for a moment that he was doing anything more than if he had been dealing with horses or gold and silver. Public sentiment was not enlightened, although the Gospel has always struck at the very root of slavery. The essence of the Gospel is that we are to do to others as we would that others should do to us. Nobody would wish to be another man's slave, and therefore he has no right to have another man as his slave. Perhaps, when Onesimus ran away and came back again, this letter from Paul may have opened Philemon's eyes a little as to his own position. No doubt he may have been an excellent master and trusted his servant. He may not have treated him as a slave at all, but perhaps he had not regarded him as a brother. Now Onesimus has come back and will be a better servant, but Philemon will be a better master, and a slaveholder no longer. He will regard his former servant as a brother in Christ.

Now, this is what the grace of God does when it comes into a family. It does not alter the relations. It does not give the child a right to be pert and forget that he is to be obedient to his parents. It does not give the father a right to lord it over his children without wisdom and love, for it tells him that he is not to provoke his children to anger, lest they be discouraged. It does not give the servant the right to be a master, neither does it take away from the master his position or allow him to exaggerate his authority, but all around it softens and sweetens. Rowland Hill used to say that he would not give a halfpenny for a man's piety if his dog and his cat were not better off after he was converted. There was much weight in that remark. Everything in the house goes better when grace oils the wheels. The mistress is, perhaps, rather sharp, quick, tart; well, she gets a little sugar into her constitution when she receives the grace of God. The servant may be apt to loiter, be late up of a morning, very slovenly, fond of a gossip at the door, but, if she is truly converted, all that kind of thing ends. She is conscientious and attends to her duty as she ought. The master, perhaps—well, he is the master, and you know it. But when he is a truly Christian man, he has a gentleness, a suavity, a considerateness about him. The husband is the head of the wife, but when renewed by grace he is not at all the head of the wife as some husbands are. The wife also keeps her place and seeks, by all gentleness and wisdom, to make the house as happy as she can.

I do not believe in your religion, dear friend, if it belongs to the Tabernacle and the prayer meeting and not to your home. The best religion in the world is that which smiles at the table, works at the sewing machine, and is amiable in the drawing room. Give me the religion that blacks boots and does them well, cooks the food and cooks it so that it can be eaten, measures out yards of calico and does not make them half an inch short, sells a hundred yards of an article and does not label ninety a hundred as many tradespeople do. That is the true Christianity which affects the whole of life. If we are truly Christians we shall be changed in all our relationships to our fellow men, and hence we shall regard those whom we call our inferiors with quite a different eye. It is wrong in Christian people when they are so sharp upon little faults that they see in servants, especially if they are Christian servants. That is not the way to correct them. They see a little something wrong, and, oh, they are down upon the poor girls as if they had murdered somebody. If your Master and mine were to treat you in that style I wonder how you would get on? How quick some are in discharging their maids for small errors—no excuse, no trying the persons again. They must go. Many a young man has been turned out of a situation for the veriest trifle by a Christian employer, when he must have known that he would be exposed to all sorts of risks. Many a servant has been sent adrift as if she were a dog, with no sort of thought whether another position could be found and without anything being done to prevent her going astray.

Do let us think of others, especially of those whom Christ loves even as He does us. Philemon might have said, "No, no, I don't take you back, Mr. Onesimus, not I. Once bitten, twice shy, sir. I never ride a broken-kneed horse. You stole my money. I am not going to have you back again." I have heard that style of talk, have not you? Did you ever feel like it? If you have, go home and pray to God to get such a feeling out of you, for it is bad stuff to have in your soul. You cannot take it to heaven. When the Lord Jesus Christ has forgiven you so freely, are you to take your servant by the throat and say, "Pay me what you owe?" God forbid that we should continue in such a temper. Be pitiful, easily entreated, ready to forgive. It is a deal better that you should suffer a

wrong than do a wrong, much better that you should overlook a fault
that you might have noticed than notice a fault that you ought to have
overlooked.

> Let love through all your actions run,
> And all your words be kind,

is said in the little hymn that we used to learn when we were children.
We should practice it now, and

> Live like the blessed virgin's son,
> That meek and lowly child.

God grant we may of His infinite grace.

I want to say this, and then I am done. If the mysterious providence
of God was to be seen in Onesimus getting to Rome, I wonder whether
there is any providence of God in some of you being here tonight! It is
possible. Such things do happen. People come here that never meant to
come. The last thing in the world they would have believed if anybody
had said it is that they would be here, yet here they are. With all manner
of twists and turns they have gone about, but they have gotten here
somehow. Did you miss a train, and so stepped in to wait? Does not
your ship sail quite so soon as you expected, and so are you here
tonight? Say, is that it? I do pray you, then, consider this question with
your own heart. "Does not God mean to bless me? Has He not brought
me here on purpose that this night I may yield my heart to Jesus as
Onesimus did?" My dear friend, if you believe on the Lord Jesus
Christ, you shall have immediate pardon for all sin and shall be saved.
The Lord has brought you here in His infinite wisdom to hear that, and
I hope that He has also brought you here that you may accept it and so
go your way altogether changed.

Some three years ago I was talking with an aged minister. He began
fumbling about in his waistcoat pocket, but he was a long while before
he found what he wanted. At last he brought out a letter that was well
near worn to pieces. He said, "God Almighty bless you! God Almighty
bless you!" And I said, "Friend, what is it?" He said, "I had a son. I
thought he would be the stay of my old age, but he disgraced himself
and went away from me. I could not tell where he went, only he said he
was going to America. He took a ticket to sail for America from the
London docks, but he did not go on the particular day that he expected." This aged minister bade me read the letter, and I read it. It was
like this: "Father, I am here in America. I have found a situation and
God has prospered me. I write to ask your forgiveness for the thousand
wrongs that I have done you and the grief I have caused you, for,
blessed be God, I have found the Savior. I have joined the church of

God here and hope to spend my life in God's service. It happened thus: I did not sail for America the day I expected. I went down to the Tabernacle to see what it was like, and God met with me. Mr. Spurgeon said, 'Perhaps there is a runaway son here. The Lord call him by His grace.' And He did." "Now," said he, as he folded up the letter and put it in his pocket, "that son of mine is dead, and he is in heaven. I love you, and I shall do so as long as I live because you were the means of bringing him to Christ."

Is there a similar character here tonight? I feel persuaded there is—somebody of the same sort. In the name of God I charge him to take the warning that I give him from this pulpit. I dare you to go out of this place as you came in. Oh, young man, the Lord in mercy gives you another opportunity of turning from the error of your ways, and I pray you now here—as you now are—lift your eyes to heaven, and say, "God be merciful to me a sinner" (Luke 18:13), and He will be so. Then go home to your father and tell him what the grace of God has done for you and wonder at the love that brought you here to bring you to Christ.

Dear friend, if there is nothing mysterious about it, yet here we are. We are where the Gospel is preached, and that brings responsibility upon us. If a man is lost, it is better for him to be lost without hearing the Gospel than to be lost as some of you will be if you perish under the sound of a clear, earnest enunciation of the Gospel of Jesus Christ. How long halt some of you between two opinions? "Have I been so long time with you," says Christ, "and yet hast thou not known me?" (John 14:9). All this teaching and preaching and invitation, and yet do you not turn?

> O God, do thou the sinner turn,
> Convince him of his lost estate.

Let him linger no longer, lest he linger until he rue his fatal choice too late. God bless you, for Christ's sake. Amen.